Ezra DeFreest Simons

Divine Pictures of the Christian Centuries

Ezra DeFreest Simons

Divine Pictures of the Christian Centuries

ISBN/EAN: 9783337780029

Printed in Europe, USA, Canada, Australia, Japan

Cover: Foto ©Thomas Meinert / pixelio.de

More available books at **www.hansebooks.com**

OF THE

Christian Centuries.

BY REV. EZRA D. SIMONS.

TROY, N. Y.:
WM. H. YOUNG, 214 RIVER STREET.
1875.

CONTENTS.

I.

THE DIVINE ARTIST.

The Pictures drawn by divine hand. Mystery of the book of Revelation. Line of interpretation. Gibbon an involuntary witness. Evidence of fulfilled prophecy. Need of intelligent faith in the Scriptures. Direct objects of the Apocalypse. The transcriber of the visions. Why he was chosen. Circumstances. The voice of the Divine Artist. His qualifications declared. Vision of the Divine Artist. His characteristics indicated. Effect of vision upon John. The Divine Christ. Revelations for all men. He might picture all our personal future.................... 24

II.

LETTERS TO THE CHURCHES.

Interest in reception of letters. The character of the writer connected with this. How important is a letter from Christ. For us personally. Location of churches originally addressed. Seven-fold representation of Jesus. Seven-fold description of the churches. Mingled praise and blame. United threatenings and promises. Direct application of the letters..................... 50

III.

THE OPENED DOOR AND UNSEALED BOOK.

Language of Revelation emblematic. Right of private judgment. Opened door. Throne. Rainbow. Elders. Four beasts. Who do these denote? Orders of redeemed souls. Lightnings. Thunders. Voices. Lamps of fire. Sea of glass. The sealed book.

The worthy Lamb. The unsealed book. Horses. Seal first broken. White horse and crowned rider. Seal second. Red horse. Seal third. Black horse. Seal fourth. Pale horse. Seal fifth. Martyrs. Seal sixth. Dreadful picture. All these fulfilled. Seal seventh. Lesson of faith. Future of God's people in hands of Christ as the Lamb of God.................................... 78

IV.

THE SOUNDING TRUMPETS.

Connection between Broken Seals and Sounding Trumpets. Form pictures of entire political history of the Christian Centuries. Use of trumpet. Two groups of trumpets. Strange answer to prayer. The historic test of book of Revelation. Sounding of first Trumpet. Fearful hail storm upon the earth. Second Trumpet. Burning mountain cast into the sea. Third Trumpet. Star falling upon rivers. Fourth Trumpet. Sun smitten. Fifth Trumpet. First woe Trumpet. Sixth Trumpet. Period of impenitence... 107

V.

THE MIGHTY ANGEL AND SEVENTH TRUMPET.

The Mighty Angel. From heaven. The Great Reformation. Little book. New world. Seven thunders. Strange oath. Little book eaten. Temple and altar measured. Two witnesses. War against these. Dead and risen. Effect of their resurrection. Time of the power ruling in the great city. Temporal power of Pope ended. The Seventh Trumpet. Far reaching in its notes. Accumulating evidence of the inspiration of the Scriptures. If true in prophecies, true in what it declares of experimental religion. Encouragement for Christians........................ 139

VI.

THE GLORIOUS WOMAN AND WARRING BEASTS.

Comprehensive sketch of ecclesiastical history. Early age of church. Woman. Birth of New Testament. Efforts of Satan to destroy this. Second period of church history. Moral conflict. Third period of church history. Flight of true church into the wilderness. The deceptions of Satan. General description of the exile of the church. The first beast pictured. Source. Power of. End of first beast prophesied of. Second beast. Council of Trent. Authority of beast. How maintained. How used. Its name. Papal church not the true church, nor the historic church. Continuance of ecclesiastical Rome not defined by numbers. The two horns; one, the "Episcopal" church. Series of visions. New song. Gospel angel. Babylon doubly fallen. Worshipers of beast to be punished. Blessed to die in the Lord. Reaping time of the world. Warning. Encouragement..................... 173

VII.
THE SEVEN LAST PLAGUES.

Means of overthrow of Papal power. Number Seven. Term plague. Origin of the Plagues. God praised for using these. Seven angels of Plagues. Upon earth. Noisome sore. Upon sea. Naval conflict. Upon rivers and fountains of waters. Blighting sun. Plague upon seat of beast. Drying of the Euphrates. Three devilish spirits. The place of gathering. Plagues poured upon the air. Great city divided into three parts. Great hail. Side scene. The large number of symbols fulfilled. Seven Plagues all inflicted, destroying the temporal power of the Pope. God's hand in history executing judgment.............................. 211

VIII.
THE BABYLON-WOMAN.

Retrospect. Ecclesiastical Rome. New Era. Vatican Decrees. Claim of Infallibility. Babylon-woman. Imposing appearance. Name. Position. Association with kings. Effect of this. Corruption of city of Rome. Woman in wilderness. Scarlet colored. Full of names of blasphemy. Attire. Cup in her hand. The Mystery. Drunken. Picture of Papal church as now seen. Explanation of angel. Epitome of Romish history. Spiritual fall of Babylon-woman predicted. Reasons for overthrow. Character of Popes. Effect of her downfall. Manner of the final destruction. To be identified with the Pope and city of Rome. Nothing strong or abiding except it be the right. Warning................ 246

IX.
THE GREAT CONFLICT.

Picture of the Present. Our direct interest. Conflict preceded with shout of victory. This shall embrace the perfection of the church of Christ. Feelings of Apostle. Worship God! Vision of embattled hosts. Army of good. Great leader. His names. His weapons. Our part in the strife. The forces of evil. Conflict moral. Peculiar place of. Battle cry. Result of the Conflict. Aim at human soul. Battle-ground of heart. Who are you serving? A plea for Christ.................................. 274

X.

THE MILLENNIUM.

In the future. Glory of, unquestioned. Meaning of the term. Extent of time. Sabbath-age. Overthrow of Satan. By divine power. Resulting condition. All upon earth then may not be Christians. Positive feature. Rule of the martyr-spirit. Resurrection of the body does not then take place. Peculiar type of piety. The second-coming of Christ not yet. Elements of martyr-spirit. Righteous may die natural death. "Blessed the dead who die in the Lord henceforth." No war. Final Conflict. Resurrection. Judgment. Standards of. Final condition of the Impenitent. Nature of punishment. Appeal................... 301

XI.

THE REDEEMED WORLD AND GLORIFIED CHURCH.

The new heaven and earth. General view. What and where is that world? Question of renovated earth. Human life transfigured. No sea. Possible destiny of matter. Danger of literalizing the symbol. That world a reality and place, though wholly spiritual. Special abode of the glorified church of Christ. Blessed condition of this. Free from the ills of the present world. Promise and warning. The inheritance of all things. The New Jerusalem. Particular view. Picture, not of heaven, but of glorified church. Application of details. Renewed danger of literalizing. Closing lines. Worship. Finality of the Revelations. "Come!" Only Jesus. "Come, Lord Jesus." 329

PREFACE.

I send forth this volume on the great sea of literature, hoping for it a prosperous voyage; and that into whatever homes or hands it may enter, it may carry a blessing.

THE AUTHOR.

I.

The Divine Artist.

Revelation, Chapter 1.

THE heavens are aglow with perpetual splendors. Shining sun, glinting stars, fair moon, and glowing planets, wide spread constellations, trailing comets, falling meteors, have in all ages attracted heavenward the eyes of men; while cloud by day and night, the sheen and flash of lightning, the crash and roll of thunder, have added to the wonders of the sky.

But these have chief bearing upon the earth as such, and upon us as material beings; declaring, indeed, to our minds and souls, "the glory of God, the firmament showing his handiwork, day unto day uttering speech, and night unto night showing knowledge," and "there is no voice nor speech where their language is not heard." But God has made the heavens to shine with other splendors, to be pictured with symbols more mysterious, at the time, than the stars have been; he has spread above the earth, in the sight of man, portraitures of the future—some, dread, fearful, as awful as his judgment and indignation; some, bright with glories surpassing fairest sunrise or most gorgeous sunset scene—bright with the splendors of his throne and of the city of gold.

Human wisdom should never have traced these, as by no laws within our control could man have mapped the things which the divine hand caused to pass, in dioramic view, before the eyes of a wondering man. At best, man could only tell of them when seen. Men can measure the distance of the sun and planets and a few of the fixed stars; they can weigh in their mathematical balances the worlds, and give the size of these; they can declare accurately when eclipses shall take place, and comets return from their wanderings; but they have no means of their own to foreknow and describe in advance the events of human history—politically, socially and morally; one with divine vision alone can foresee, and only a divine hand can portray beforehand what the time to come shall bring forth.

Indeed, divine power and wisdom have to do with those things which are chiefly the carrying out of his own plans. To foretell, may be but to disclose a purpose formed embracing the things revealed.

We should only expect outlines, not full drawn pictures; yet definite enough to make it possible to recognize the things represented when these should appear; for the portrait and object portrayed must be alike in the main features if they belong to each other.

There has always been a mystery about the book of Revelation. Doubtless, there was such to him who first saw the wondrous visions of this. There is such now about parts of the book, for there are prophetic symbols not yet fulfilled; and until the great Artist shall point us to the rapturous realization of the last chapters, will mist and darkness keep us from seeing clearly the meaning of some of the portraitures. To many, to most, to almost all minds, the whole book seems to be sealed. If they look at it, it is with a hopeless feeling that it cannot be understood; as if it was never intended to be more than read. Many fail to read it altogether, except they turn to the closing portions descriptive of the New Jerusalem, unmindful that this is the only distinct book of the Bible upon reading which a blessing is pronounced. "*Blessed is he that readeth,*" is among the opening lines. Perhaps, some have thought that a course of lectures upon it would scarcely be profitable or interesting, that something more practical would be better; but, in addition to the fact that this is a real part of the word of God and so should be unfolded, is the added blessing pronounced: "Blessed are they that *hear* the words of this prophecy." I ask you, then, to hear attentively and earnestly and for yourselves; for so shall you, according to the promise, be blessed. If you judge that there is nothing practical here, mark the words, "Blessed are they who *keep* those things which are written therein."

I am not to deal in fanciful interpretations, pleasant or plausible imaginings; but to point you to the fulfillment of much of the book, to the fac-similes of most of its symbols; for it is a fact that a careful study of this has convinced many that the key to its storehouse of meaning has been found. Those who have shared with you in the feeling that all was mist and darkness, have discovered the solid basis in fact; the pictures have become realities which may be plainly recognized.

As illustrating God's wondrous way of working, of using instruments least likely, it has been ascertained that Gibbon's "History of the Decline and Fall of the Roman Empire," is the best commentary in existence, in the way of facts, upon an important part of the book—from the sixth to the ninth chapters. No one will suspect that the skeptical Gibbon, eminent as a scholar, and, in some respects, with no superior in all the ages as a historian, would shape his material designedly to favor the Bible; yet, the facts he gives, form a true counterpart, in character and order—so far as his work extends—with the symbols of Revelation. Other works as reliable, afterward take up the thread of historic interpretation and afford us the true explanation of the symbols; so that the confirmation rests upon grounds which all are bound to accept.

One of the strong evidences of christanity and of the inspiration of the entire Bible, is the fulfillment of scriptural prophecies, of the Old Testament and the New. Daniel's prophecies of the very time when Christ should appear and be cut off for the transgressions of the people, were strictly realized, and many other inspired predictions of the prophets have come to pass.

The prophecies of Christ and of the apostles have been and are being fulfilled; of the former, not alone as to the destruction of the temple at Jerusalem, but as given symbolically in the book before us. Mathematical demonstration is here permitted in some instances, and if calculation should not be exact always, it might be owing either to uncertainty of ancient dates or to a choice between several events closely related.

In these days, when—as in other times—so many assaults, from so many directions, are being made upon christanity, and especially upon the key to our whole position—the Bible, it is highly important that you should be intelligently grounded in your faith in the word of God. You need to feel, as you rightly may, that your position within and behind this is impregnable. To know that prophecy has been fulfilled, that the book of Revelation is being verified by actual history, will aid in strengthening your confidence in the Book of God. Daniel and Ezekiel had visions of some of the same great realities pointed out in Revelation, which accords with the linking together of all truth in the Old and New Testaments; prophecy, as other things, blending, since they came from the same source, and make up the one grand whole.

The direct objects of the book are evidently to give comfort and support to God's people in all their tribulations, and especially at those times when it should seem as if things were working against the cause of Christ—pointing with instruction from the present to the great future; so, however dark it might seem now, light should appear ahead; however confused present affairs might be, order would at last come forth; though defeat and death should overtake God's people, his kingdom should move on and in the end triumph. These objects did the book serve at first with the early church; these objects was it intended to meet in ages to come; and, if we will read the great conflict of moral forces now going on in the political, intellectual, ecclesiastical, and moral world, in the light of the revelation of Jesus Christ, confidence and hope shall be experienced by us. Well may it be said in view of all, and at the very outset of the revelation, " Grace be unto you, and peace." We shall see, thus, that it is not simply a conflict waged between man and man, the issue of which depends upon the greater human wisdom or might of the parties; but, that the angels are, also, interested in the strife, and are having part in this—the good against the bad; and that the Lord God is the leader of his hosts against the prince of darkness and of evil: so the result shall not be uncertain; it has already been pronounced.

The person used to transcribe the prophetic visions displayed by the great Revealer, the divine Artist, was the "beloved disciple" and apostle, John. He was now an old man. Sixty years of the ninety of his life had been passed in the service of his master. For preaching the gospel he was seized by the Roman power, during the persecution of the disciples in the reign of Domitian, and sent in exile to the desolate isle of Patmos, in the Ægean sea. The rocky heights of this were to be made, by the revelations given, more glorious than Sinai when this burned as with fire beneath the presence of Jehovah.

The first christian century was drawing to its close,

and with it the labors of the last of the apostles, and the final revelation in word from the Lord Jesus to men. Because he was the only surviving apostle, he may have been appointed to view and to write of the wonderful visions from heaven; but, there was, also, a fitness of character and a ripeness of christian experience which eminently fitted him for the sight and the task. He was honored of Christ when on earth, by being of the chosen three who were permitted to behold the display of his greatest power, in raising from death to life, as in the case of the dead maiden; to witness his chief glory on the Mount of Transfiguration, and his extreme anguish in Gethsemane; and, of the three, he was pre-eminent for mental attainment and for heart devotion. Of all the disciples, most intimate with Christ before his death, he was made to look in upon the glories of heaven after this, and to see the things which should be "hereafter." "He bare record of the word of God, and of the testimony of Jesus Christ, and of all things that he saw." With the same fidelity which marked his writing of the life of Christ, and his unfolding, in his epistles, of the heart of christianity, which is love, did he now pen the visions granted to him. He had always had to do with inner spiritual realities and glories; he was now brought most fully into the presence of these.

Think of him as an old man, with the peculiar glory of old age upon him; moreover, as a ripened christian; banished to Patmos for his devotion to Christ; not morose, but filled with the love of Jesus, and not separated from him because removed in person from his brethren, for Patmos was as near to Jesus and heaven as Ephesus. It was the sabbath, "the Lord's day," the name then given to the first day of the week, the day of Christ's resurrection; and, then and thenceforth, the christian sabbath. Whatever the particular day may have been in its natural features, and though the place of his confinement was drear, all was glorious within his soul. He was "in the spirit on the Lord's day." This invested his mind and heart like a robe of beauty; it filled him, like the fragrance of the flowers; it gave pure and blessed life to his faith and hope and love, as did the pure air from the sea invigorate his aged body. He is walking forth, not to look upon the rocks or seas, but in loving worship of God. Was he thinking of the time when Jesus called him at the sea of Galilee? Was he recounting all that wondrous life of his Master? Did he remember Calvary, and the glories of that first christian sabbath, when Jesus—"risen indeed"—appeared to the disciples? Did he recall when Jesus was taken up from the presence of the apostles into the opening heaven? Was he looking back in heart over the record of Christ's loving goodness to him through all the years of his christian life? He was, probably, thinking, too, of that band of christian brethren at Ephesus, and of the churches to whom he had ministered in other places. He, doubtless, was mindful of the promises of Jesus, and his heart was looking up. In the wisdom of Christ he was now "able to bear" more than could have been well told him in the other days of their communing. It had required years of prayer and labor and trial to make him ready for the coming disclosures; and when his enemies sent him to Patmos, Christ's hand was in the event, overruling their evil for his own great and gracious purposes.

It was under these circumstances that the Revelation was made, the divine pictures spread forth; not necessarily all on one day, but on successive days, as he was able to view the symbols and to record these. But the opening vision was on the sabbath spoken of, at which time came to him,

First: The *Voice of the Divine Artist.*

The bearing of this and of what immediately followed, was, doubtless, to inspire not only the apostle's confidence in the subsequent disclosures, but to present to us and to all to whom these should come, the *reasons* why we should credit them. In what John heard, do we learn these: A voice as of a trumpet—clear, distinct, silvery, firm, great, sounded behind him, "saying, I am alpha and omega, the first and the last; and what thou seest write in a book and send it unto the seven churches which are in Asia." These and all his opening words unite in declaring the *qualifications* of Christ for his work as revelator, whether in word or symbol. These are, that he is,

1. The "faithful witness," in which character he had come into the world, even "to bear witness unto the truth." Such he continued to do from the opened heavens which shone about Patmos with a sabbath peace and blessing. As a witness, to him had been made known the things of which he was

to testify. In the subordinate position which he voluntarily assumed in taking upon him his office and work as mediator and savior, he is represented as receiving even his knowledge from the Father; so, in the case before us, we read that this is "the revelation of Jesus Christ which God gave unto him, to show unto his servants." He is a divine witness, then—a witness of divine truth, and as such, are we to accept the entire book of Revelation from him.

2. But he is, also, "the first-begotten of the dead." Thus is he a *living* witness, and possessed of all the meaning and prestige of that wondrous event, his resurrection; and of the fact, growing out of this, that all the dead shall eventually rise.

3. He is "the Prince of the kings of the earth," and as such is qualified to declare the events of human history, and even to shape these according to his will, and to carry out his own great and gracious purposes; for the kings of the earth should be subject to him, as subjects unto a sovereign.

4. Not only faithfulness and life and power fitted him for the work of revelation, but his love to us and gracious work wrought for us, qualified him; so

that we may gladly say, "unto him that loved us, and washed us from our sins in his own blood, and hath made us kings and priests unto God and his Father; to him be glory and dominion forever and ever."

5. His second coming is given as a pledge of his ability to bring about the very things he has declared. "Behold, he cometh with clouds; and every eye shall see him, and they also which pierced him; and all kindreds of the earth shall wail because of him." Certainty, finality, of word and deed, is connected with this. Hence is it said, "Even so, Amen."

6. But he is the "Alpha and Omega, the beginning and the ending." He has the whole cycle of human history in his hands. He was at the beginning of all, and will be at the ending. The circle, commencing at his throne, and sweeping around the globe in all time, shall come back again to his feet; and is, in its entireness, at all times, before him.

Every qualification is, then, declared of him;— fidelity, life, power, love, justice, and eternal connection with all things. Thus, in word, is Christ presented, giving authority to John to write and send the message of the things he should see to the churches.

The voice was followed by a *Vision of the Divine Artist.*

We are not to understand that the forms of Christ's appearances were literal. That he really appeared, is true; but the forms representing him were according to his character or his relation to special events or things. The representation here is specifically in view of the revelation he was to make; and answered, in another form, the same purpose which the words already explained served.

From the twelfth to the twentieth verse he is represented,

1. As being in the midst of his churches, called the "seven golden candlesticks," maintaining by his presence the light of these; pouring in the oil of his grace and spirit, his truth and love, and keeping these, as did the priests the lights of the golden candlestick in the temple, perpetually burning. Great need had the churches of this assurance, then as now; for the fierce winds of worldly influence and persecution should threaten to extinguish the light of the churches of Christ. But the light of his truth should never go out. Some torches might wax dim and be even cast down, but others should

remain steadfast. If the seven churches of Asia should cease to burn and illuminate the world, before passing, other lamps should be lit at their fires; and, so, the light should continue. He then fed the lamps afresh and was in the midst of the seven golden candlesticks to do this especially, with the oil of revelation, which has not yet been exhausted, nor—anymore than the rest of his Bible— ever shall be. The sun and the stars have not burned with a truer or more unwasting brightness than have the truth-fed golden candlesticks. These have been hidden, indeed, as the other, by clouds or in eclipse; but they have endured as ever, and have come forth from between the clouds or from behind the eclipse, hailed with greater joy because for a time lost sight of.

2. He has the "seven stars" of the churches, or ministers of these, in his right hand. He uplifts them before the world. If the world or churches become "star" worshipers or idolaters, he will suffer the objects thus regarded to be humbled, or will blight them, causing them to pass from the sight of men like lost stars in the heavens. But, in all their true service of him, does he make them to be like planets

reflecting the light of the sun, guiding them by his spirit, binding them to his heart by the power of this as the mighty law of gravitation, the planets to the great solar center; protecting them, upholding them, causing them to shine with the luster of his truth, to the praise of his glory and the good of his churches, and of a world darkened by the night of sin and unbelief.

3. The "garment" flowing down to his foot was not priestly but kingly in its make, exhibiting him as royal in his authority as revelator; the "golden girdle" being the symbol of his strength and preparation for his work as such; his "head" and "hairs white like wool, as white as snow," displaying his wisdom, being venerable in this as "the ancient of days." His "eyes were as a flame of fire," far-seeing, penetrating, carrying with them the power to look into the darkest places and hearts, and to disclose all hidden things, "running to and fro into all the earth"—the symbols of his omniscience. "His feet were like unto fine brass," showing the firmness and uprightness and righteousness of his doings, in all his goings forth; as pure his feet in their course as "fine brass burned in a furnace."

His voice was "as the sound of many waters," being expressive of his great and far reaching authority; "out of his mouth" proceeding "a sharp two-edged sword," of his truth, which is "sharper than any two-edged sword, piercing even to the dividing asunder of soul and spirit, of joints and marrow, and is a discerner of the thoughts and intents of the heart;" while "his countenance was as the sun shineth in his strength," so glorious and light and life-giving in its power.

We wonder not, as Christ was thus personified, that even John should "fall at his feet as dead." If he was at first bewildered, if he did not so far recognize his tender, loving Master, surely his heart regained its strength, when the kind touch of the Savior's right hand, which he had felt in other days, rested upon him; and the voice which had stilled the tumult of the storm on Galilee by its authority, and had calmed the fearing hearts of the disciples by the loving assurance, "It is I; be not afraid," now said, "Fear not; I am the first and the last"—the same now as then, "he that liveth," as in the days of incarnation; "and was dead, and, behold,

I am alive forevermore, Amen; and have the keys of hell and of death."

In all this, there was a reproduction in part of the scene on the mount of Transfiguration. So, in the appearance of Christ, in its effect upon John, in the touch and loving words of the Savior; and the united features of the vision disclose him—here as there—as the *divine Christ*, the Lord of heaven and earth, of his churches and ministers. His "excellent glory" was his fitness as a Revelator.

As thus seen let us not lose sight of him in all that follows. This manifestation was intended as an introduction to all else, and was necessary to all else; and is the most important part of this introductory lecture.

While the revelations made to John, and for the seven churches of Asia because of the apostle's direct connection with these, which would ensure their reception and careful preservation, the unfoldings were for all the churches of Christ in all time; for the number "seven" denoted completeness, entireness, and the seven churches were the representatives of the whole church of Christ, always. So are they for us; and be it ours to give heed to them as if addressed to the churches of Troy, N. Y., and, distinctively, among others, to the Vail Avenue Baptist Church.

These great things have to do with us. They are taking place, some of them, now; and in the time to come, in this world and hereafter, we shall be witnesses of their reality. We have a personal concern in them. Christ comes, as John saw him, to this church. May he walk among us, and kindle anew to a living flame his truth here, and make us personally and as a church as lights in this community; holding us in his right hand that we may reflect his glory.

He has your future in his hand, and might show it to you in word or symbol; but while he has not judged best to describe particularly the coming events of our individual lives, he has revealed our destiny as being governed by our moral condition, and has made known the way of salvation and of life to us. O! be guided by the light of his truth to his cross, that you, being saved, may be sanctified in the truth; and come with joy into the presence of his glory, and not be of those "who shall weep and wail because of him."

II.

The Letters to the Churches.

Revelation, Chapters 2, 3.

EVEN in these days, when, through the ready means of transportation and cheap rates of postage, letters are carried to almost every door—the masses availing themselves of this way of communicating—there is the keenest interest on the part of every person in the reception of such. The post-man is, in the eyes of the people, one of the most important public servants. Indeed, he always was; from the days when messages were sent by couriers, or were intrusted to private carriers; to the time of that most wondrous institution, the mail-coach, the arrival of which was the event of the day or week; until the era of the mail-train, when huge bags, filled with letters, aggregating tons in weight, are hurried across a continent or from end to end of the land, and when letters find their way, transported by steam, the world over.

The interest in the letter received is graded by the position or character of the writer, or his relation to us, or our interest in him. If we should receive a favorable letter from the President of the United States or the Emperor of Germany or the Sovereign of England, we should be highly elated, and would read and re-read line after line until we knew the contents by heart. If the letter were on business that concerned our welfare, or the interests of a nation or of the world, a sense of responsibility would be created in us; if the letter breathed of love, contained wise instruction, faithful warning, and great promises, our hearts would be touched and our lives affected. If the permit were inserted to enter the Presidential mansion as a special friend, or the royal palace as an honored guest; if a promise of honor, of wealth, of adoption, of high position—if possible, of life, were given—all, in words and sentences breathing personal, special love, as from our best and most loving and loved friend; surely, the most lasting and good effect would follow.

Such are the letters of Christ to the churches. They come from one more exalted than President, or Emperor, or King; from one whose interest in us is most tender, and true, and loving; who sends messages such as our best earthly friend, however wise or wealthy or loving, though seated upon the highest places of earth, could not truthfully indite. Christ, the great Revealer, the Divine Artist, precedes his pictorial revelations with the evidences of his direct and most thorough interest in those to whom these are made. Though employing an amanuensis, in accordance with a common practice in ancient times—one not yet passed away—the letters are as from his own hand.

A letter is most interesting to us when it is for us, for us personally. The letters of Christ were addressed to each of the churches in their independence; and, that we might be assured that they are, also, for us individually, and as a church, and for every one and every church, each letter closes with the earnest line: "He that hath an ear, let him hear what the spirit saith unto the churches." This means all, this means each; for it reads not, "*They* that have ears, let *them* hear;" but, "*He* that hath an ear, let *him* hear."

Let us now open Christ's letters to us and earnestly read them, seeking to learn and apply their contents. The letters will be found to conform to a general arrangement, although the substance of each was suited to the particular church addressed. You may run iron into a mould, and taking out the casting you may run brass into the same mould; or, gold; or, silver. So, there is one model after which the letters are formed, which will enable us to do in one lecture what we might well take seven for, to treat of these together; and the variety in the substance will enable us to select that which is best suited to us.

I. We will first glance at the *places* where were the churches originally addressed by the Lord Jesus Christ.

They were all in Asia. This name is now given to the largest and most densely peopled continent on the globe. In former time it had a much more restricted application, and comprised only the western part of what is now known as Asia Minor. It was a province of the Roman Empire, bequeathed to Rome by a prince who held dominion over it.

Ephesus was the capital. This was an important city, commercially and politically. Here was the celebrated temple of Diana; and, here, where the silver shrines were made, because of loss in the sale of which by the spread of the gospel, Paul's companions were seized, at the instigation of Demetrius, and a great uproar was had. Paul labored here three years, publicly and privately—from house to house, not shunning to "declare the whole counsel of God," nor ceasing "to warn every one night and day with tears." Timothy was afterward pastor of the church here, at the time when Paul's letters were addressed to him; the church finally coming under the oversight of the beloved John.

Smyrna was situated some forty miles north of Ephesus, and was, also, an important city commercially. It was once destroyed by the Lydians, and remained desolate some four hundred years, after which it was re-built by Alexander the Great. It was, likewise, destroyed by an earthquake in the year 167, A. D., and again restored, and remains until the present, being now a city of some 130,000 inhabitants; and instead of being on the decline, is improving. The celebrated Polycarp was here martyred, and is supposed to have been the angel, or pastor, of the church at Smyrna when the letter was sent by the Savior to this. When he was arraigned before the Roman pro-consul at Smyrna, and his death was demanded, the Jews being most active in seeking this, he was called upon to curse Christ; upon which he replied: "Six and eighty years have I served him, and he has done me nothing but good; how then shall I curse him? my Lord and Savior? If you would know what I am, I tell you frankly, I am a christian."

Pergamus was once noted for its temples, its literature, and arts. A temple of Diana was here located upon an eminence. A library sustained here was removed by Antony to Alexandria in Egypt, and became part of that famous library which was subsequently, with such loss to the world, destroyed by the Turks, on the plea, that if there was anything in the books contrary to the Koran, they ought to be destroyed; and, if they agreed with this, they were not needed.

Thyatira was located on a plain environed with mountains, and was noted for the business of dyeing. It was the home of Lydia, mentioned in the book of Acts, "whose heart the Lord opened."

Sardis was the residence of Crœsus, celebrated

for his wealth, "as rich as Crœsus" being an adage not yet fully passed away. The place was once taken in war by Cyrus, and near it Xerxes encamped on his way to Marathon. The people were in ill-repute among the ancients because of their voluptuousness. It was destroyed by an earthquake in the time of Tiberius and was rebuilt by this Emperor. It is desolate now. Two columns and a few remains of ancient buildings, one of which is thought to have been built some three hundred years after the building of Solomon's temple, alone continue to the present; a solitude oppressive and saddening to the mind being said to brood over the site.

Philadelphia was some twenty-five miles from Sardis, and was the second city of Lydia. It was, also, subject to earthquakes. It is now a Turkish town, and was the last of the cities of Asia Minor to yield to the Turkish power, in the year 1400, A. D. It was called "city of God," and was situated on four hills, from which a grand view of natural scenery was had. There are some 3,000 houses in it now, all but 250 being occupied by Turks.

Laodicea was a place of considerable wealth; but

was like other places in this region, repeatedly visited by earthquakes, which almost completely destroyed the city and caused this to be abandoned.

Gibbon writes of the end of all these places, as seats of christian churches, as they appeared in the 15th century:

"Two Turkish chieftains, Sarukhan and Aidin, left their names to their conquests, and their conquests to their posterity. The captivity or ruin of the seven churches of Asia was consummated; and the barbarous lords of Ionia and Lydia still trample on the monuments of classic and christian antiquity. In the loss of Ephesus, the christians deplored the fall of the first angel, the extinction of the first candlestick, of the Revelation; the desolation is complete; and the temple of Diana, or the church of Mary, will equally elude the search of the curious traveler. The circus and three stately theatres of Laodicea are now peopled with wolves and foxes; Sardis is reduced to a miserable village; the God of Mahomet, without a rival or a son, is invoked in the mosques of Thyatira and Pergamus; and the populousness of Smyrna is supported by the foreign trade of the Franks and Armenians. Philadelphia alone has been saved by prophecy or courage. At a distance from the sea, forgotten by the emperors, encompassed on all sides by the Turks, her valiant citizens defended their religion and freedom above four-score years; and at length capitulated with the proudest of the Ottomans. Among the Greek colonies and churches of Asia, Philadelphia is still erect, a column in a scene of ruins; a pleasing example that the paths of honor and safety may sometimes be the same."

II. In the letters to the churches in these places we find a *seven-fold representation of Christ*. In each case he declared some characteristic of himself, bearing upon the peculiar circumstances and condition of each, the very presentation of himself in such lights being calculated to arouse special attention to himself and his message, and to awaken their consciences. These representations pointed in part to his appearances as John had seen him.

To the church at Ephesus he wrote as the one who holdeth "the seven stars in his right hand," and "walketh in the midst of the seven golden candlesticks." They needed to remember this, as we shall see—to consider that he had power over minister and church, and could work his own will against or for them. To the church at Smyrna he spoke as "the first and the last, which was dead and is alive." They required for their help, the great and comforting assurance that he was the living Jesus. The church of Pergamus was pointed to "the sharp sword with two edges" proceeding out of his mouth. The church at Thyatira was addressed by him as the "Son of God, who hath his eyes like unto a flame of fire, and his feet are like fine brass." Here he proclaims his divinity, and his searching view of all things, and the pureness and uprightness of his going forth in blessing or in judgment. Unto the church at Sardis he appealed as having "the seven spirits of God, and the seven stars," the seven spirits standing for the perfect Holy Spirit who can at the same time move and work in different directions, in each and all of the churches at once. To the church at Philadelphia he represents himself as the "holy" and "true," as "he that hath the key of David, he that openeth, and no man shutteth; and shutteth, and no man openeth," the latter being the expression of his authority and power, in providence and by his word and spirit. To the church at Laodicea he was "the Amen, the faithful and true witness, the beginning of the creation of God." What he said was a finality, and he is faithful and true as a witness, and is the head of the church, as he was the head of the creation of God; "for by him were all things made that are made." We shall find that all these features were appropriately mentioned, and that in the characteristics specified, he did work among the churches.

Which of these developments of his nature and offices is best suited to us, as a church and as individuals? Or shall we say, let Him appeal to us in all his characteristics?—Let Christ be to us "all in all?" The Lord open the eyes of our understanding that we may see in what respects we need Christ, and make us willing to hear his voice however sharp this may be, cutting right and left—though used in love; and to endure the searching glance of his eye; and to have his footprints upon our hearts, though his "feet" be as a "refiner's fire, as the purifier of silver." We say, come, thou who holdest the seven stars, and hold thy stars here in thy right hand; come, thou who walkest amid the seven golden candlesticks, and let us "see thee in the sanctuary," and in our homes and on our streets, walking in the midst of this thy church and of all thy churches. Wield thy sword, thou living Jesus, and send forth thy spirit; and open the door of mercy so that no man can shut this, thou holy and true one; and be thou the head of this thy church, O thou Amen—Christ, faithful and true, the "beginning of the creation of God."

One thing is most certainly adapted to us—that seven-fold declaration of Christ, made to each and all the churches in precisely the same words: "*I know thy works.*" Yes, Christ knows the works of this church; knows them positively, knows them fully, knows their nature, knows their extent; knows how many are working for him, and how much, and the motives in which we are working—whether it is that man should know them, or content that God knows them. Does he know them to approve them and us; or, the contrary?

III. That he knew their works is attested by the *seven-fold description* he gave of their condition. He might make an equally explicit statement of ours.

The church at Ephesus had suffered trouble, and was patient; it could not "bear them which are evil;" it put to the test, doubtless in connection with the word of God, those who falsely claimed to be apostles or teachers, and found them "liars." The church had borne, and had been patient—the language is repeated, and for Christ's name's sake had labored, and had not fainted. They had among them the Nicolaitanes—errorists, whose false doctrines were manifest in evil deeds, and these the Ephesians hated. They bore with their doctrines but hated their deeds. The church at Smyrna was suffering tribulation and poverty; but, said Jesus, "thou art rich," "rich in faith." Those who claimed to be Jews and were not the Israel of God, but were really of "the synagogue of satan," were their enemies; yea, satan himself should work against them. Ten years—or ten prophetic "days," were they to suffer; which took place during the Diocletian persecution which lasted that time. Their condition was pre-eminently one of suffering and destitution; yet, that these things are not so bad as some others, not so bad as error, or indifference, or sin, is seen in the fact that the church at Smyrna is the only one of the original seven which has continued in any form unto the present time.

The church of Pergamus was located where was the stronghold of Satan, and they had among them those who held "to the doctrine of Balaam, who taught Balak to cast a stumbling-block before the children of Israel, to eat things sacrificed unto idols, and to commit fornication"—persons, who while pretending to be good, enticed others to evil. Those who held to the doctrine of the Nicolaitanes— a doctrine not known now, were, also, here. Thyatira was known for its "charity, and service, and faith, and patience, and works, and the last to be more than the first;" they having grown in these. Yet they suffered a false prophetess, named after the Jezebel of ancient time—noted for her fanaticism and profligacy, to teach doctrines alluring and vile in their tendency. Some among them held to the doctrine; others did not, these not knowing "the depths of satan." The church at Sardis had a name to live but was dead. In one sentence, the cold, formal, professional church, is set forth; possessed at best of only a few sparks of the christian life. The church at Philadelphia had a "little strength," had kept Christ's word, and not denied his name, notwithstanding the Jews, of the synagogue of satan, here as elsewhere, had arrayed themselves against the church of Christ.

The Laodicean christians were "lukewarm," "neither cold nor hot;" yet were saying: "I am rich, and increased with goods, and have need of nothing," not knowing that they were "wretched, and miserable, and poor, and blind, and naked." They were not simply in this unworthy condition, but were, also, self-deceived, flattering themselves that they were otherwise.

If our church were to be named after either of these churches, what should it be called? Perhaps, we shall be able better to answer, as we get further along, passing to notice,

IV. The *mingled praise and blame, the commendation and reproof*, pronounced by the Lord Jesus Christ upon the churches.

1. There was commendation given in every instance but one, the church at Laodicea, whose pride connected with indifference, prevented the first word of approval. Christ was always ready to commend when this was due. Not that he ever flattered.

Flattery, and sincere praise wisely expressed, are two different things. There is an old saying, "He that flatters you is either a knave or he thinks you a fool." To speak an honest word in favor of another might oftener be done than it is. We leave such things too frequently until our friends die, when our words can do them no good. One well-timed sentence of appreciation spoken in the living ear, is better than a tomb-stone covered with eulogistic inscriptions; the one is golden, the other, like marble. Christ is more ready and better pleased to laud than to censure, as he is readier to bless than to inflict judgment.

For their labor and patience, and zeal for righteousness and truth; for the trueness of their motive and their persevering courage, did he commend his people at Ephesus. Only words of approbation and encouragement did he have for his disciples at Smyrna, who were so true amid all their tribulation and earthly poverty. The church at Pergamus was praised for its steadfast devotion to the name and faith of Jesus, though they were environed by satan himself, and one of their number, the faithful Antipas, had been martyred for Christ's sake. The growing charity, and service, and faith, and patience, and works, of the church at Thyatira were all extolled; and even Sardis, though indirectly, was gently commended because there was some good remaining among them; and the disciples at Philadelphia had, though weak, kept Christ's word and confessed his name, and for this were credited in his account with them. How good if only words of approval could have been spoken of all!

2. But, otherwise was the case. There was *deficiency* on the part of almost all, and the word of faithful love must needs be spoken. "Faithful are the wounds of a friend," and faithfully did Christ deal with his people; yet with a wisdom divine. The words pointing out their defects were not those of one who delighted in reproving. We may take a secret delight in telling others of their faults; not so, with the Lord Jesus, but, as our imperfections cause him pain, so does reproving these distress him.

You will ask, after the many words spoken in favor of the church at Ephesus, what is lacking in this? Hear the words of Jesus: "Nevertheless, I have somewhat against thee, because thou hast left thy first love." They were outwardly right and devoted; but the heart had lost the warmth and fervor, the strength, and steadfastness of its first love to Christ; when the spirit of sacrifice and obedience had marked them in the sight of God and of men. Shall we name our church after the church at Ephesus? The church at Pergamus endured error of doctrine leading to error of life, and for this it was rebuked. The people of Thyatira were reproved for like evil. The church at Sardis was condemned for its formality, being dead while professing to be alive. The reproof of the church at Philadelphia was indirect, and was pronounced, by implication, upon its deficiency in strength; while the church at Laodicea, the only one of which no good was spoken, was severely condemned for its lukewarmness, because it was neither cold nor hot. Shall we surname us after Sardis or Laodicea? Let us be faithful with ourselves in the matter, and hear what follows:

V. The *united threatenings and promises of the Lord Jesus.*

The Ephesians were threatened with the removal of their candlestick out of its place, with the extinguishment of the light of the church, which was equivalent to the destruction of this. He who represented himself to this people as walking amid the golden candlesticks thus applies this manifestation of himself, and threatens them according to their condition; for if their first love which they had lost should not return, if the love of Christ thus dying down—and love forever grows or decreases—should cease, their spiritual life would end; and, in time, the body itself, without a soul, should perish. But if they would "do their first works," expressive of their first love, the promise was that he would give them "to eat of the tree of life, which is in the midst of the paradise of God;" so, nourishing their spiritual life with heavenly food. It is a sad truth, that there is no evidence of lasting repentance on their part; that neither threatening nor promise availed, and the church perished. Splendid churches were afterward built, outwardly there was seeming prosperity; but the Mohammedans triumphed over them, and the word of Jesus was so faithfully carried out that the skeptical historian Gibbon remarked it. This specific judgment was more fully executed upon this church than upon any other of the original seven, not one trace of it remaining, and for centuries not one christian was found in the place. Dreadful warning this to us now, for churches at this day and in this land have died out, for the one reason above all others, that they lost their love to Christ, that love without which grand church edifices are only magnificent mausoleums, entombing the dead body of the church.

No threat was made to the church at Smyrna. This needed none. The people were devoted to Christ at every sacrifice and in all their suffering, and only encouragement and promises were given to them. "Fear not;" "Be thou faithful unto death, and I will give thee a crown of life." "He that overcometh shall not be hurt of the second death;" thus appropriately did the living Jesus speak to those who, for their trueness to him, were being exposed to, and were, in some instances, suffering literal death. He who declared to the church at Pergamus that he had the "sharp sword with two edges;" threatened to "fight against them with the sword of his mouth," if they repented not. A most fearful thing this, for to have Christ fight against us were worse than to confront the world or satan, since he is mightier than they; and for him to turn his truth against us were most dreadful, as it is most blessed to have this on our side. But if they overcame the temptation to "eat of food sacrificed to idols and to commit fornication," he would give them better food, "even to eat of the hidden manna," of the bread of heaven; and would bestow the sign of favor and the pledge of good, in the "white stone" with the "new name" written therein. Dishonor, suffering and death, were pronounced against those of Thyatira who yielded to Jezebel—to idolatry, by him who "with eyes like unto a flame of fire" "searcheth the reins and hearts," and who with "feet like unto fine brass" comes in righteousness to "give unto every one according to his works;" but Christ would raise those who overcame such things and "kept his works unto the end," to great power and honor, and give them "the morning star" of his own light and glory and exaltation; for he afterward declared, "I am the bright and morning star."

The church at Sardis having a name to live, though really dead; having only a "few names which had not defiled their garments"—their low condition being reached through positive sin—was told by him who held the seven spirits of God and the seven stars, that if they repented not "he would come on them as a thief in the night," and would despoil them. But the overcoming ones should be "clothed in white raiment," and he would not blot out their names from the book of life, but would confess them before his Father and his angels. The threat was of outward judgment, which probably came to them, and as suddenly as the earthquake which executed his will upon them. There is no direct threatening against the church at Philadelphia, but there is the promise from him who was holy and true, who had the key of David, and so full authority in his kingdom, that he would make the overcoming ones "pillars in his temple," and grant to such to be special bearers of the name of God. But the Amen—the decisive one, the faithful and true witness, the head of all things, threatened the church at Laodicea with shame and ill if they turned not from their lukewarmness. The church here having suffered through an earthquake, the people had been indifferent to re-building a sanctuary, and to the promotion of the cause of Christ; and he stood at their door and knocked, and if they opened he would enter to bless, and if they overcame their half-heartedness and became decidedly his, he would grant them to "sit with him in his throne, even as he also overcame and was set down with his Father in his throne."

Thus did Christ appeal both to their fears and hopes, working first upon the one, then upon the other; but in all, even in his rebukes, assuring them of his love. His word again and again was: "As many as I *love* I rebuke and chasten." Were they tempted to rebel against the threatenings? Love should still their rebelliousness, or make them doubly guilty for not heeding the faithful words.

How is it with us! Has not Christ "somewhat" against us; a few things? The word "somewhat" is not in the original, the true translation being, "I have against thee;" as if he spoke decisively; not falteringly, but faithfully and "with authority, and not as the scribes," telling us our faults plainly. Is there no lack of love among us? Is there no sin in our hearts? No error in our minds? No evil in our lives? Are we lukewarm? Then saith the Lord Jesus, "Let him that hath an ear to hear, hear what the spirit saith unto the churches." The spirit appointed to "take of the things of Christ and show them unto us," speaks for Christ unto his churches now; and the same threatenings hang over us as were made to the churches of Asia. The churches to which the letters were directed, and in part, the places where they were, have passed away; but the epistles remain, and the Holy Spirit continues and brings them with original force to all churches in like conditions. It is for us, then, to repent, to turn from all our sins and failings to the Lord Jesus with sorrowing hearts and renewed consecration and love. Especially so since such glorious promises are added, given in every instance to those who "overcome" the evil; being always personal—to "*him* that overcometh."

I have not failed to see that every letter was addressed first of all to the "angel" of the church, to the pastor; that he should faithfully communicate the will and word of Christ to the people; moreover, applying to himself first of all that word. What a responsibility! I would meet it to-night. While in the name of the Lord Jesus I commend you for all the good you have done, I declare in faithfulness that the Lord Jesus has "somewhat against us." The two things most fearful of all, I think, are held against us—we have "lost our first love," and are "neither cold nor hot." I point you to the dreadful fact that in both such instances the destruction of the churches was threatened—God would put out the light, or would spew them out of his mouth. Let us be warned; especially, let us turn from all wrong, in view of the exceeding great and precious promises of Christ.

"He that hath an ear to hear, let him hear what the spirit saith unto the churches." That means you, too, who are unconverted. Does Christ know the condition of his people? So does he know yours—how great are your sins and unbelief. Has he "somewhat against" his own? How much more against you? Shall he threaten his professed disciples; and does he spare you? Not so; but his justice and wrath are pronounced against you, more fearfully than against his church. But, oh! I am permitted to hold forth his promise of pardon and of eternal life, which shall be yours if you will repent and believe on the Lord Jesus Christ. Read the threatenings, hear the promises, obey the word of the gospel of Christ! "Blessed are they that *read*, and *hear*, and *keep* the words of the prophecy of this book."

III.

The Opened Door and Unsealed Book.

Revelation, Chapters 4–8: 1.

ONLY as we remember that much of the language of the book of Revelation is emblematic, that the visions were symbols, shall we form any just or satisfactory conception of the things presented; yet the pictures are faithful representations of realities. They do not always stand for persons, but sometimes for qualities of being, and for events as well as things. Of course, no one will claim, except it may be the Pope; no one can rightly claim, not excepting the Pope, infallibility in the interpretation of the book of Revelation, any more than of the other parts of Scripture. In all explanations of this we recognize the right of private judgment; and reverently should we submit all our views to the great Teacher and Revealer of truth, who has written unto his churches, praying him to lead us by his spirit "into all truth."

I cannot enter minutely and at length into every passage and symbol of the book. That would be to present to you a commentary upon this, instead of giving you lectures with a more general scope, which is my plan.

Let us not forget the two great persons who had chief part in the revelations made, the great Revealer, the divine Christ; and the Holy Spirit, by whose presence and influnce John was enabled to view the things portrayed, for it is said again and again, that he was "in the spirit" when he saw and heard these wondrous things.

Look first toward the *opened door*.

Only, as it were, a door separates earth and heaven, this world and the worlds to come. Day by day is it now opened; "he who openeth and no man shutteth," keeps the passage way to heaven open to his people; but we see it not with bodily vision. The spirit, released from the body, passes through it into the presence of the realities, more glorious than the symbols upon which the apostle looked, and for which these in part stood.

Looking through the opened door, a view of the dazzling throne of God greeted John, and the undescribed and the indescribable one, the Eternal Father, was seen clothed in garments of light, pure and brilliant. A "rainbow," the sign of peace, of hope, of promise, overarched the throne, revealing this as a throne of grace. Round about the throne were four and twenty other thrones, or seats—the word being the same as that translated throne just before; and four and twenty elders sat thereon. Were these the representatives of all those who, overcoming every evil, should be granted to sit down with Christ in his throne? Were they the elders of Israel, the most worthy of patriarchs, and prophets, and apostles of Christ?—the foremost of the saved in the Old and New Dispensations? This would accord with other representations in the book of Revelation. That they comprised redeemed souls, appears from the song they afterward sang to him who had redeemed them by his own most precious blood. Granted that the text of the chorus is in part questionable, as found in the English version; yet the fact that they were "clothed in white raiment"—"the white raiment is the righteousness of the saints;" and, "had on their heads crowns of gold," given, as we may well believe, in accordance with divine promise, again and again spoken, shows them to have been the personifications of "the church of the first-born, which are written in heaven."

Moreover, that they were not angelic dignitaries is seen in the *order* of the singing, "the voice of many angels round about the throne," following that of the beasts and elders, the latter singing of love redeeming, while the others sang in general praise. It is a beautiful arrangement that the angels should *surround* the redeemed host of heaven; as if, unlike the elder son of the parable who coveted the greater honor, they accorded the chief place to the lost sons found; and enclosed them more safely in the heavenly world, by angelic power, as they are seen subsequently to guard the gates of the city of the New Jerusalem.

They were, then, the embodiments of those who were permitted to be nearer the throne than others; just as the truest explanation of the four beasts, or, living creatures, in the midst and round about the throne, is, that these are the likenesses of those, who, redeemed, have, because of their christian fidelity, been privileged to be nearest the eternal throne. These, with the courage and strength of the lion, had been conquering ones on earth; like the bullock, burden and yoke-bearing and patient, they had endured for Christ's sake, and when they had long served, had been led to the sacrifice, but were now raised to their reward by the hand of God; with the intelligence of manhood, and with the rapidity of the eagle, they had served God heretofore, and now reverently and humbly, with ever watchful eyes, as they looked forth and beheld the evidences of God's glory—in his works and ways, and saw other souls enter heaven; did they with tireless voices proclaim his praise, or were ready to go forth to do his bidding. The great truth was thus set forth that there are orders of redeemed souls in heaven; and that our places there shall be determined by our christian courage and achievement, our burden and cross bearing, our growth in the knowledge of Christ and readiness in his service, here. To such is it given, according to divine and gracious promise of reward and honor, to be nearest the great white throne and him that sitteth thereon; and to lead forever in the high praises of God and of the Lamb.

Merely to gain heaven for safety's sake, is not the highest ambition of the christian; but, to occupy by God's grace an advanced place there. This be our aim and effort. There is a throne and a crown for thee, my brother; a place in the midst of the throne for all true christian heroes. Shall we gain it? "Of gold, and silver, and precious stones," must we, then, build upon the only true foundation; that our works as well as our souls may abide in the day of fire.

From the throne of God, as John beheld this, shot forth "lightnings"—symbols of his justice, and rolled forth "thunders"—booming warnings, and came forth "voices"—speaking the divine invitations, and pleadings. "Seven lamps of fire" were burning before the throne of God, which represent the seven spirits of God, or the complete, perfect, Holy Spirit, whose workings are, indeed, like fire— enlightening, purifying, searching, warming, sanctifying, melting, consuming; and thus doing the will of God in all the churches at once, operating with seven-fold forces in each of the seven churches then; and in all, now. Before the throne was a "sea of glass," the shining pavement of heaven, on which pure and peaceful surface walked the heavenly hosts, whose chief occupation is to "give glory, and honor, and thanks, to him that sitteth on the throne, who liveth forever and ever"—all the service and joys of heaven, having this as their blessed key-note.

But all this is the back-ground of a scene which now appeared before the eyes of the apostle. In the right hand of him who sat on the throne was a book, a scroll, written within and without—a thing unusual, for it was the wont of men then to write on only one side of the parchment; and the book was sealed with seven seals—again that complete number, setting forth completeness of contents, the book being the *great volume of the Future.* Here had been already penciled God's foreknowledge of the events of all the future of earth; and, here, inscribed his great and far reaching purposes, already formed. "A strong angel with a loud voice proclaimed, Who is worthy to open the book and to loose the seals thereof?" "And no man in heaven nor in earth, neither under the earth, was able to open the book, neither to look thereon." Neither can we see before us into the future, nor shape its events; this is all a sealed book to us, except as God himself provides a way to open it.

John wept much because no man was found "worthy to open the book, neither to look thereon." As he wept one of the elders said: "Weep not, behold the lion of the tribe of Judah, the root of David, hath prevailed to open the book, and to loose the seven seals thereof"—the strong and conquering one, the royal one, who had "prevailed" in the conflict of his earthly life, was able to open it. But as John looked to see the lion of the tribe of Judah, he "beheld, and, lo!"—he was surprised, for he saw not the form of a lion, but "in the midst of the throne and of the four beasts, and in the midst of the elders"—for he was the center of even these and of the throne itself—"stood a *lamb* as it had been slain, having seven horns and seven eyes, which are the seven spirits of God, sent forth into all the earth," the Holy Spirit being represented by the latter as subject to Christ in his work. The Lamb of God, as slain, the crucified but living Redeemer, with the strength and courage of the lion and the innocence and worth of the sacrificial lamb, who, as the Lamb was the Lion, came and took the book from the right hand of him who sat upon the throne; and, as he did so, beasts and elders fell down in worship before him, and a new song was sung in heaven: "worthy is the Lamb!" Angels took it up, "ten thousand times ten thousand, and thousands of thousands;" and earth caught the strain as this floated down the heavenly heights; the whole universe swelled the chorus of the grand oratorio: "Blessing and honor, and glory, and power, be unto him that sitteth upon the throne and unto the Lamb, forever and ever." The heavenly songs commencing here run through the book of Revelation, and the anthems of joy, from first to last, are poured forth to Christ.

II. Behold, now, *the unsealed book.*

As each seal of the book was broken, the scroll within was unrolled; and the things that appeared were evidently pictured, and passed before the eyes of the apostle as a panorama. The first four scrolls were adorned with forms of horses. There was, doubtless, a special design in this, the image conveying a definite idea, and possessing a particular meaning then. However unforeseen were the events symbolized, the symbols would make a precise impression. At one time they might represent war, at another rapid marches, at another burden-bearing or racing. The intent of the symbol would be in accordance with the most marked service to which the horse was put at the time the emblem was given. Both scriptural and classical references present it as then representing *war, fleetness* and *strength*. The events symbolized should be warlike; material or moral conquest should take place, and other things be done in which the horse should be used—things passing with the rapidity and strength of the horse.

We should expect from the gradual unfolding of the seals, that the events foreshadowed would be progressive. The horses were seen going forth, at times from conquering to conquer, as should the events pass gradually on. Moreover, we should judge that the epochs of history would follow each other; that, while they might grow out of each other, the second should begin after the first commenced; the third, thus, to succeed the second; and so on to the last seal broken.

Remembering that these are ideal symbols; that while Christ is said to have unrolled the book, he, the Divine Artist, pictured the scenes before the eyes of John—which is the meaning of the representation—behold now,

Seal *first* broken.—As the Lamb broke this, John "saw and behold a *white* horse; and he that sat on him had a bow; and a crown was given unto him; and he went forth conquering to conquer."

It is natural to ask what was the significance of this color of the horse? what special meaning did this have? White is the emblem of "innocence, purity, prosperity." White horses were used by the ancients on occasions of state and victory. In triumphal processions, the conqueror was drawn by white horses; on marriage parades and coronation displays, these were again selected; besides which, the white horse was supposed to be capable of greater speed than others: so, used as a symbol, it would convey the idea of prosperity, of rapid and far extended triumphs.

The things revealed were to begin to come to pass "shortly" after the revelation was made. As the providence of God would have it, the historian Gibbon, singularly enough, takes up the history of the Decline and Fall of the Roman Empire at about the time John wrote his wonderful visions. We are thus enabled without any intention to this effect, on the historian's part, to learn from his writings whether anything transpired soon after the Revelation was made, which answered to the symbol of the white horse, and to the other successive representations.

The very year in which the book of Revelation was written, A. D., 96, marked an epoch in the history of the Roman Empire. Domitian, called by Gibbon, "a cruel tyrant, the last of the twelve Cæsars," died, and a new period was opened by the accession of Nerva, "noted for his virtues," a "great general and popular Emperor," under whom the Empire attained its greatest dominion. In A. D., 117, Adrian became emperor, able and devoted to the true interests of the Empire; while Antoninus Pius and Marcus Aurelius Antoninus, the one in the year 138 and the other in 161, followed, and by their wise administration of the government, prolonged an era of the greatest prosperity to the year 180 A. D. This period is called by Gibbon distinctively an "age," the "age of the Antonines;" and is placed by him foremost in the annals of the world's history, in the remarkable words: "If a man were called to fix the period in the history of the world, during which the condition of the human race was most happy and prosperous; he would, without hesitation, name that which elapsed from the death of Domitian to the accession of Commodus." Virtue and wisdom characterized the exercise of power, the armies were well regulated, the laws respected and justly administered, the emperors honoring liberty and not using their great power despotically. On the banks of the Danube and the Tigris rode the white horse from conquering to conquer, new nations being added to the Empire. The "bow" and the "crown" had a significance then which they could have had only in that period; for the bow was not a usual Roman weapon, but was Cretan, and was appropriately used only because Nerva was a Cretan by birth; and the crown of laurel then worn was soon replaced by the jeweled diadem. If the symbol disclosed by the breaking of the first seal had been formed after instead of before this period it could not have been more expressive.

But, in a manner characteristic of prophecy, the symbol bears a double reference. As the prophecies of the Old Testament relate both to the nations then existing, and the gospel dispensation to be brought forth; and, as the prophecy of Christ mingled its declarations of the destruction of the temple at Jerusalem and the end of the world: so, does the symbol of this first seal have a double bearing; for while so truly applicable to the period named, in its outward circumstances, it, also, sets forth the rapid and far spread triumphs of the gospel which then took place.

Once again, as we see farther on in Revelation—ch. 19: 11—did the "white horse" ride forth, and "he that sat upon him was called Faithful and True, and in righteousness he doth judge and make war." In this instance, it is to final conquest, and victory, and judgment, that he moves; for "he was clothed with a vesture dipped in blood;" but in the case before us he goes forth to conquer simply the hearts of men. "From conquering to conquer" did he ride—as if, as it has been well said, "he had conquered in his death and resurrection, and will conquer" in his work as the living Jesus.

The gospel was spread with marvelous rapidity then. Its triumphs in the first century, during the lives of the apostles, were great; but they were far surpassed now. Where before it had been received, it was now welcomed more fully; and in all directions, to the most distant parts, did it gain the most astonishing victories. It moved like an army with banners, led by the "Captain of Joshua's host," who in olden time had led his people to the conquest of Canaan; and who now on white horse, as a conqueror, sped the arrows of conviction into the hearts of millions. A large proportion of the Roman Empire became professed christians. Persia, Hither India, Mesopotamia, Armenia, Arabia, Asia Minor, Greece, Italy, Germany, Spain, Gaul, Britain, Egypt and Northern Africa, were the scenes of its triumph. Some of these countries had numerous churches and were "full of Christians." These were everywhere aggressive. Missionaries, no more than merchants, travelers, and other private individuals, sought to lead men to Christ; all, even female captives, were busy telling of Christ's love to sinners. The very number of Christians made it a matter of policy with Trajan and Adrian to shield them measurably from the wrath of their enemies. To have photographed the spread of the gospel then, would have been to produce the picture of a white horse with crowned and armed rider,

5

going "from conquering to conquer;" and the first-sealed scroll is verified, is broken and reproduced in history, in fact.

Behold seal *second* broken.—As the hands of the Lamb of God broke this and unrolled the second scroll, there "went out another horse that was *red: and power was given to him that sat thereon to take peace from the earth,* and that they should *kill one another :* and there was given unto him *a great sword.*"

Red was the symbol of devastation, of war, of bloodshed. The period of peace and prosperity just spoken of, was to be done away with, was to be "taken away," doubtless, in such a marked manner as to be distinctly traced; and internal, civil war should follow, for they would "kill one another;" and the sword wielded should be "great," as expressive of the great slaughter which should occur.

Was this realized? For, remember we are dealing with facts, not fancies; historic facts, related to us by one who was not prejudiced in favor of christianity, yet who stated general facts as he knew them, truly. We find from history that the death of Marcus Antoninus, and the accession of Commodus, A.

D. 180, marked a new era in Roman history, an era extending some eighty or ninety years. It was a time of civil war; the Romans "killed one another," some thirty emperors and twenty-seven pretenders to the Empire violently supplanting each other. Whether the symbol was intended to cover the whole of this period, or whether other seals embraced a part of it, it was certainly appropriate to the first portion of it—from the time that the weak Commodus yielded to the thirst for blood, and, when civil war sprang up and prevailed.

As even before the sun rises in the east, the reflection of his beams may be seen on the western hills; so, before the time came for men actually to see these things, were they illumined with the light of Revelation: but it was as if only the red rays were reflected.

Seal *third* broken.

When the Lamb had opened the third seal "lo, a *black* horse," was seen, "and he that sat on him had a *pair of balances* in his hand; and I heard a voice in the midst of the four beasts say, A measure of wheat for a penny and three measures of barley for a penny; and see thou hurt not the oil and the wine."

The color of this horse denotes distress and calamity. In scripture it is used for fear, famine, and death. The "scales" were the symbol of justice or equity; but when used to measure corn or food, they were the emblem of scarcity, or it might be of exaction. This is the idea advanced here; for a great rise in the price of provisions is set forth, and an appeal is made to the people to be careful of their vines and olive trees, and all waste was to cease. This might grow out of or be associated with burdensome taxation, which would lead the people to destroy their vines rather than be oppressed.

Such a condition of things did exist in the Empire, and contributed to the downfall of this, in the judgment of Gibbon being closely connected with this. The people were taxed most exactingly, and an edict was issued, that "If any one shall sacrilegiously cut a vine, or stint the fruit of prolific boughs, and craftily feign poverty, in order to avoid a fair assessment, he shall immediately on detection, suffer death, and his property be confiscated." The greatest distress accompanied these exactions. Brutal punishments were inflicted on the people, many being made to suffer death, mendicants alone escaping;

and these were ordered to be gathered, placed on board a vessel, and taken to sea and drowned.

If this whole feature of Roman history were in its substance or meaning, as it transpired, thrown upon canvas, we should have the picture of a black horse with a rider thereon, bearing a pair of scales. This is the picture Revelation gives, true to the facts.

Seal *fourth* opened.

When the fourth seal was opened, "behold, a *pale* horse: and his name that sat on him was Death, and hell (or hades) followed with him. And power was given unto them over the fourth part of the earth, to kill with the sword, and with hunger, and with death, and with the beasts of the earth."

• The word pale here means pale green or yellowish green, and represents the reign of death, as paleness is one of the features of this. But it would be death not so much through war as by disease. There are four ways in which it is here set forth; death by sword, by famine, by death or pestilence, and by wild beasts, the latter three growing out of, or attending the first; as famine, pestilence, and, in some places, the ravages of wild beasts, result from war.

All this we find confirmed by facts. A period from A. D. 243–268, follows that of the exactions of the last mentioned phase of Roman history, and corresponds with the symbol opened by the breaking of the fourth seal. It was the time of the first Gothic invasion of the Empire, the Goths, in the year 250, coming down the Danube, passing around through Greece, and approaching nearly within sight of Rome itself. In the sack of one city alone, 100,000 persons were put to death. Both from foreign invasion and domestic strife, were multitudes destroyed with the sword. This was not all. Gibbon says: "This gloomy period of history has been decorated with inundations, earthquakes, uncommon meteors, and preternatural darkness, and a crowd of prodigies, fictitious or exaggerated. But *a long and general famine* was a calamity of a more serious kind. It was the inevitable consequence of rapine and oppression, which extirpated the produce of the present, and the hope of future harvests." So, they were "killed with hunger." They were, also, to be killed with Death, the sombre name given to pestilence. Of this Gibbon writes: "Famine is almost always followed by epidemical diseases, the effect of scarcity and unwholesome food. Other causes must, however, have contributed to the furious plague which, from the year 250–265, raged without interruption in every province, every city, and almost every family, of the Roman Empire. During some time 5,000 persons died daily in Rome, and many towns that had escaped the hands of the barbarians, were entirely depopulated. Half of the population of Alexandria perished; and could we venture to extend the analogy to the other provinces, we might suspect that war, pestilence, and famine, had consumed, in a few years, a moiety of the human species." History speaks, also, of wild beasts, which at this period extended their devastations.

For an artist with the keen eye and skilled hand of a Nast (think of a Nast, the most wonderful caricaturist of the age, inspired of God!) to have drawn an emblem of that time, he should have penciled no more faithful symbol, than that of the pale horse with Death as its rider.

Seal *fifth* opened.

When the fifth seal was broken a vision was seen of the martyrs before the altar of God, as if their blood, like Abel's from the ground, cried from beneath the altar of sacrifice, unto God on behalf of their brethren. The evident intent of this vision was to display an age of *martyrdom*, which should succeed the last period and the others noticed.

Do we find anything which accords with such a representation? Again the symbol is a faithful shadow cast upon the page of Revelation by a reality—the reality being seen in advance only by the divine mind, the sunlight of his wisdom alone sufficing to create the shadow, before men beheld the substance. Diocletian became Emperor in the year 284, and reigned until A. D. 304. It was in this period that one of the notable persecutions of christians by the Roman government took place. It was the tenth that came from this quarter, and was the last directly from this, being designed so to be. A great, a universal, effort was purposely made to destroy completely and everywhere the christian name even. In its magnitude and severity, it surpassed any that preceded it. The prisons were crowded with christians: the rack, the scourge, the iron hook, the red-hot bed; fire, steel, savage beasts and more savage men, were made to do, and did their utmost to annihilate christianity in all the Roman Empire. The effort proved a failure, confessedly so; for Galerius, who instigated Diocletian to commence the persecution, himself published an edict of toleration, and requested christians to pray for the public welfare.

When the *sixth* seal was broken, the wonder of John was anew excited; and, now perhaps more than ever; for the scene made visible was more fearful. This is pictured in the 6th chapter, v. 12–17.

This representation, like the others, was symbolical. The mistake has been made to suppose that it was literal, and referred to the end of the world; whereas, like the images disclosed by the opening of the other seals, it is the reflection of a definite period of history, one following that of the fifth seal and coming before the seventh. The whole symbol betokens *consternation, commotion and changes.* The "earthquake" is most frequently used in scripture to denote the agitation and breaking up of nations; "sack-cloth," sadness and distress; the "moon red like blood," war; "stars of heaven," princes and rulers; the "departing heavens," revolution in high places; and "mountains" and "islands" moving out of their places, great convulsions in the political and moral world: all of which was fulfilled soon after the Diocletian persecution.

When Constantine ascended the throne, there was a turning and overturning. Other Emperors were put out of the way; the Roman Eagle gave way on their ensigns to the cross; the capital was moved to Constantinople, a city newly built, and which had never known the pagan idols; and the form of government was altered. "Heathen augurs and soothsayers, were suppressed; heathen priests and magistrates were removed; heathen temples were demolished," and "a new religion, and a new order of things arose in the world's history." While to make the period doubly true to the symbol, after the time of Constantine, but in the same century, the Huns and Goths threatened the Empire; their approach being preceded, in the year 365, by an earthquake most fearful and destructive, which shook the greatest part of the Roman world. In Alexandria alone 50,000 persons lost their lives by the incoming and outgoing of the waters of the sea. Consternation was spread by these things among all classes of the people: an awful realization of a most dreadful picture.

A momentary change now takes place, connected with the last scene and the one to follow. The winds which threaten the world are restrained as by four angels. A command comes forth from another angel, to check the winds until the servants of God are sealed—sealed, that they might be known and be safe in the day of danger; the winds referring to the hordes of enemies on the borders of the Empire, who, strange to say, when the invasion took place, were careful to spare christians. The true servants of God were sealed with the truth, through the teachings of good men, against that time of trial which marked the union of church and state that took place, in one form under Constantine, when with the multitude who were led by patronage and worldly favor to join the church, increased error and worldliness poured into this.

That the Huns were stayed on the borders of the Empire, is a fact; and the word of God was fulfilled amid the acclaims of angels. Though the number sealed was comparatively small — 144,000—it was seen to be only a part of an innumerable company who out of every nation should be gathered with all the martyrs, to hunger and thirst and suffer no more; "for the Lamb which is in the midst of the throne shall feed them, and shall lead them to living fountains of water, and God shall wipe away all tears from their eyes."

One more seal remained to be broken. "And when he had opened the *seventh* seal, there was silence in heaven about the space of half an hour." There was pause as if one series of events had ended, and another was to commence, the two blending. With the notice of the one, I now close.

I point you in conclusion to the historic confirmation of the word of God, to the very fulfillment of its symbols; and so direct you to the lesson of faith in God and his word.

It is a marked feature of the book of Revelation that so often the addresses are personal; as if the disclosures, with their lessons, were not simply for the church of Christ as a whole, but for distinct churches, and for individuals; so, the lesson of faith taught by the scenes of the Opened Door and Unsealed Book, is for each child of God; and, as we are enabled to trust Christ for the unfoldings of history, we are, also, permitted to resign to him our personal lives. Our future is not uncertain; it is before God as if it were *now*. The book has been written before him, every line fully inscribed, and the proof-sheets are already in the hand of Jesus. I repeat, in *the hand of Jesus*. In his keeping, as the Lamb of God, has it been placed; and his personal worthiness, what he has done for us, and all his great dealings in the world, inspire fullest confidence in him. That he so loved us as to give himself for us, is the pledge of our safety and good. Love that sufficed to lead him to die for us, is adequate to all else; and, we know that while the book is in his hand, and is opened by him, and for his sake, and in his interests, nothing shall befall us at variance with our redemption, with our being kings and priests unto God, and our final triumph over all evil.

However varied are the unfolding records, as gradually the seals are broken, all is fully under Christ's direction, under his charge as our loving and atoning Savior. To the very end of our lives shall the pages be turned by him. Not a part of the years alone, but all of these—the snowy pages of winter, the fragrant chapters of spring, the guadily embellished leaves of summer, the golden edged pages of autumn, to winters again; all shall be turned by the same divine fingers, and shall teach us what he wills, and the words shall be illustrated, with life-size pictures, in which our features shall be stamped, our homes portrayed, as by photographic art; for the book is an album as well as a history. On—beyond this life, to the glories of the resurrection, to the realities of the judgment, and the splendors of the New Jerusalem, every true christian shall be an object of Christ's special care and love. Believe it! Rejoice in it!

IV.

The Sounding Trumpets.

Revelation, Chapter 8: 2–13. 9.

AS there were seven seals broken, so were there seven trumpets sounded. I shall point to only six of these now.

There is a connection between the breaking of the seals and the sounding of the Trumpets. It appears that the book whose seals were opened was the prophetic and symbolic record of all future time; and that the contents of the seventh scroll was the seven trumpets, and these cover the outward, political, civil history of the world, until the consummation of things on earth, and the kingdoms of this world become the kingdom of our Lord and of his Christ. There is then, after this general view, a going back and taking up of ecclesiastical history, of the moral record of the christian centuries, until the New Jerusalem shall come down from God out of heaven.

The trumpet was used to herald the approach of any given thing. It made proclamation; it aroused; it sounded the charge of embattled hosts. The use of it might be specially connected with the persons whom the symbols set forth.

There is a division made between the first four trumpets and the remaining three, as if a series of four marked periods, having something in common, was to be followed by others having also something akin to each other. This very division, as we shall see, adds another evidence to the wonderful fidelity of the book before us, gives additional proof of its divine origin.

The pause, or silence, spoken of as following the opening of the seventh seal, was to end; the four winds which had been restrained until God's servants were sealed, were to be unloosed and to go forth with their fierce power upon the earth, in response to the sounding of the first four trumpets. Prayers had been offered by the saints of God that threatened evil might be averted. However earnest the prayer, it was offered in submission to God's will. "Thy will be done in earth as in heaven," mingled with the incense presented by the angel upon the golden altar which was before the throne; "and the smoke of the incense with the prayers of the saints ascended up before God out of the angel's hand." But God answered in his own way, not in the way of peace, so agreeable to the natural heart; for "the angel took the censer, and filled it with fire off the altar, and cast it into the earth, and there were voices, and thunderings, and lightnings, and an earthquake,"—pleadings with men, thunders of warning, lightnings of judgment and wrath, an earthquake of breaking up and overthrow: thus did God answer prayer then, and the trumpets commenced to sound.

According to the explanation I am giving to you of the book of Revelation, we shall look to events succeeding those symbolized by the opening of the seals, for the interpretation of the sounding trumpets; for distinct events under each of these, and for a natural grouping of the first four and the latter three. You will see that this is a searching test to which to put the word of God. It is the historic test; and, in part, it is subjecting that word to a mathematical demonstration, to which some men would prefer to subject all truth, and the results of which, so far as it can be rightly used, are accepted as conclusive. Employing the latter method, we do not always expect a strictly accurate demonstration. If the product is correct in round numbers it is true; the nearer, however, is the sum required and the sum obtained, the better will be our satisfaction.

Listen now to the sounding of the *first* Trumpet.

"The first angel sounded, and there followed hail and fire mingled with blood, and they were cast upon the earth; and the third part of trees was burned up; and all green grass was burned up."

A fierce storm was to take place, a storm of hail, accompanied by lightning, and mingled as with red snow, like blood. It was to beat upon the *earth*, as if cast upon this with fierce power. It was distinctly the earth that was to be affected; or, the people who dwelt upon the *land* were to suffer. Those things which had the strength of trees should not be destroyed in full, but all that was tender as the green grass should be burnt up, desolated.

A hail storm was generally a symbol of divine vengeance. It was so used in the plagues visited upon Egypt, when the "Lord sent thunder and hail, and the fire"—or lightning, " ran along the ground;

and the Lord rained hail upon the land of Egypt." We read in Job of "the treasure of the hail" which God declares he has "reserved against the day of trouble, against the day of battle and war." When David speaks of his deliverance from his enemies, he says: "The Lord also thundered in the heavens, and the Most High gave forth his voice, hailstones and coals of fire." The lightning is a means of destruction; red snow is a thing not uncommon in the Alps, and would be a strange but striking symbol of bloodshed. The devastation of fields, of trees, and grass, would attend an *invasion by a fierce enemy*.

Do we find anything in the natural order of events, recorded in history, which answers to this symbol? Remember, that in our last lecture we were brought by most conclusive, and, from a human standpoint, surprising resemblances between the symbols of the unsealed book and the events of history in the Roman Empire, from the age of the Antonines to the times of Constantine, from the latter part of the first to the latter part of the fourth centuries. We must, therefore, take up the connection here. So doing, we learn from unprejudiced history, that a most marked event took place early in the fifth century; commencing about the year 410, A. D. This event was the second invasion of the Roman Empire by the Goths under Alaric. He had been in the employ of the Roman Government, had sought and been refused the command of its armies; and, subsequently in retribution, had led that host which spread such consternation through the Roman Empire; and, though checked in his career of conquest then, he now, again, invaded this. The imperial court, in its consternation, moved its location, as it had done once before, this time from Milan to Ravenna. Gibbon describes the assembling of the barbarians along the coast of the Baltic, as the gathering of a "dark cloud" which "burst in thunder upon the banks of the upper Danube." The symbol set forth the bursting and beating of a thunder storm; and an unchristian historian viewing the reality without reference to the scripture, likened it to just this. A historian who wrote in that very period declares: "The sword of the barbarians destroyed the greatest multitude of men; and among other calamities, dry heats with flashes of flame and whirlwinds of fire, occasioned various and intolerable terrors; yea, and hail greater than could be held in a man's hand fell down in several places, weighing as much as eight pounds." Claudian, in a poem on this same war, likens the invaders to a *storm of hail.*

The barbarians reached Rome, and again and again laid siege to the city. The tender grass was consumed. Within the famished city, mothers devoured their own children; and pestilence with famine, did their fearful work. In the year 410, the gates were treacherously opened, at midnight, to the besieging hosts, and the doomed people were startled from their troubled sleep by the blasts of the Gothic trumpets, followed by the ravages of the conquerors. Nearly twelve hundred years after its foundation, Rome, the proud center of a world-wide power was in the possession of men, swayed by brute force, from Germany and Scythia. The havocs of that fierce storm were not limited to the city of Rome; it swept over all the provinces of Gaul. The Romans had, in the times preceding, gone up the Rhine, and had built beautiful residences and cities along the river; while others had given themselves to agriculture and horticulture: but now suddenly beat the dread tempest of war upon them; and, like the trees of the forest and the green grass of the fields, were prostrated the homes of the people. Mentz, Worms, Strasburg, Spires, Rheims, Tournay, Arras, Amiens, were either destroyed or brought under the yoke of the victors. Trees, planted and nurtured by careful hand, were literally consumed, and the fields literally wasted; while virgins and others were driven before the conquerors. It is no exaggeration to say that a third of the earth was covered with their ravages. Taking into account the three-fold division of the Empire—Eastern, Central and Western, we behold that a third of this was directly affected by the invasion. In all, we see a true resemblance to the symbol; so close, that if the "assembly" had been sounded in words instead of symbolic sounds, the gathering of the invaders should not have been more prompt, or in better accordance with the word of God.

Listen to the sounding of the *second* trumpet.

"And the second angel sounded, and, as it were, a great mountain burning with fire was cast into the sea: and the third part of the sea became blood; and the third part of the creatures which were in the sea, and had life, died; and the third part of the ships were destroyed."

What a dreadful symbol this! as if a volcanic mountain, blazing with its fires, was plucked from its bases, and hurled seething into the sea; and the waters were heated—if such a thing were possible, red hot, to blood color; and one-third of those who lived on the sea, or near its waters, or on the islands of the sea, were destroyed, and the ships were, to a third part, consumed.

The scene changes from the land to the water. What should take place would be chiefly maritime. A mountain is a symbol of great strength; thus, of a strong and powerful nation. We read in the scriptures that the "stone" which smote the image, "became a great mountain, and filled the whole earth;" the stone there referring to a kingdom. The symbol here, would, then, set forth a strong nation, filled with fiery passion, moving with impetuous fury, burning with desire for conquest, and hurled upon the sea-coasts; waging war upon the sea, and staining this with blood; and inflicting fearful destruction. War upon commerce, naval conflict, and victory at sea, is plainly symbolized.

Such a thing was scarcely to be looked for then in the Roman Empire. It was six centuries since the naval armaments had issued from Carthage to wage war upon Rome. How should such a thing now take place; or, any great power spring up at sea, to sweep the Mediterranean—the coasts and islands of this? That this sea was intended is manifest from the scripture use of the term, "the sea," or the "great sea," being then the Mediterranean.

As the waters reflect objects on their banks or surface, as the waters of the Mediterranean reflect its shores; so, look at the symbol as reflected from scenes transpiring upon "the sea." We look for these in the next notable event in the history of the Empire, after the invasion of the Goths under Alaric; and find it to be the invasion by the Vandals under Genseric, which occurred in the year 428, A. D. When they commenced their movement it was with no idea nor purpose of doing what they afterward did. Urged forward, they passed down through France and Spain to the sea coast. Invited to Africa, they crossed the straits, of Gibraltar, in boats furnished by the Spaniards, who were anxious to be freed from their presence, and by the African general, to whose aid against Rome they were moving.

The first Genseric having died, a brother of the same name, fiercer than the other, succeeded to their leadership. It is his name that comes down in history side by side with Alaric and others. Arriving in Africa, Genseric, turning from the object for which he had been invited there, entered upon the conquest of the country for himself and followers. Soon all Northern Africa was subdued by his arms, the seven provinces, from Tangiers to Tripoli, being overwhelmed by his forces, and a government being established by himself.

What should he then do? The symbol is scarcely realized yet. But let us hear Mr. Gibbon speak again. He says: "The discovery and conquest of the Black nations (in Africa) that might dwell beneath the torrid zone, could not tempt the rational ambition of Genseric; but he cast his eyes *toward the sea ;* he resolved to create a naval power, and his bold resolution was executed with steady and active perseverance. The woods of Mt. Atlas afforded an inexhaustible supply of timber: his new subjects were skilled in the arts of navigation and ship-building; he animated his daring Vandals to embrace a mode of warfare which would render any maritime country accessible to their arms; the Moors and Africans were allured by the hope of plunder; and after an interval of six centuries, the fleets that issued from the port of Carthage again claimed the empire of the Mediterranean." Sicily, the coasts of Lucania and other places soon felt their power. They sailed to the Tiber; they captured Rome, and for fourteen days, the place was despoiled by them. On the Liris, they were defeated; but the line of their operations was long, and could hardly be defended against them. A great effort was made by the Imperial court to meet and destroy them at sea. For three years vast preparations were carried forward; a fleet of galleys three hundred strong was constructed, together with transports and smaller vessels. The harbor of Carthagena in Spain, was made the anchor ground of the Roman navy. All promised well for the defeat of the Vandals; but through the treachery of Roman subjects, Genseric, guided by secret intelligence, surprised the unguarded fleet; many of the ships were sunk, or burned, or captured, and the preparations of three years were destroyed in a single day. Each spring, assaults were made by the Vandal fleet; all the coasts of the Mediterranean were ravaged, and terror was spread from the pillars of Hercules to the Nile. Surely, if ever symbol was fulfilled, this was; the waters of the Mediterranean reflecting at once the Vandal ships and the Second Trumpet.

Listen to the sounding of the *third* trumpet.

"And the third angel sounded, and there fell a great star from heaven, burning, as it were a lamp, and it fell upon a third part of the rivers, and upon the fountains of waters: and the name of the star was called Wormwood: and the third part of the water became wormwood, and many died of the waters, because they were made bitter."

We have here as a symbol, a falling meteor flashing through the sky, and coming like wormwood upon a region where rivers and fountains of waters abounded, embittering these, even imparting a deadly power. Moreover, in some sense, the meteor should be regarded as an instrument of divine vengeance, for the star fell from heaven. Taking the usual significance of the use of "star" in scripture, the symbol would display a great ruler or leader; not benignant as a fixed star, but baleful as a burning lamp. Does this symbol fit into anything which actually occurred? Was there any great leader, who, about the time last noticed—coming forward distinctly and later than the other appeared—flashed before the eyes of the world, and fell, like a meteor, upon a region where rivers and fountains of waters abounded; any besides Alaric and Genseric? We do find that such was the case—one whose name might well be called Wormwood, so bitter was his course, one who was most brilliant in his movements; *Attila, the leader of the Huns.* Although his operations were in part synchronous with Genseric, they commenced after the beginning of the latter's career, in the year 433 A. D., and were distinct from those of the other. He was accustomed to dress in brilliant colors, and claimed to carry "the sword of Mars," the god of war. His coming was like a flashing meteor; suddenly. Europe was overrun by his hordes. But it is a marked fact, that the seat of his exploits was the region of the Alps, that water-shed of Europe, where the fountains of waters are, the source of the great rivers of Europe; and that Lombardy, a country of rivers, was made to feel in an unusual manner his bitter strokes. His going, like his coming, was as a meteor; as if such had fallen into the waters, and been extinguished; for with the death of Attila, passed away the power of the Huns. He was looked upon as a means of divine judgment. He called himself, and is known in history, as the "Scourge of God." He boasted that the grass never grew on the spot where his horse had trod.

If we could have put upon the banners of Attila an emblem of his character, an insignia suitable to his army, it would have been the picture of a flaming comet or meteor; and if we should have chosen the material and color with which to have painted it, as expressive of the effect of the burning star, it would have been that of wormwood. Divine Revelation casts such upon his standard and person; and, lo! it is correct.

Listen to the sounding of the *fourth* trumpet.

"And the fourth angel sounded, and the third part of the sun was smitten, and the third part of the moon, and the third part of the stars; so as the third part of them was darkened, and the day shone not for a third part of it, and the night likewise."

This symbol shadows forth a blotting out of the present order of things in the political world, as we had occasion to notice in our last lecture, in another connection. Here only a third part is smitten; so that a third part of the sun, moon and stars, are darkened—a principal, and secondary, and still other subordinate powers, are in part eclipsed. If we take this mantle of darkness, and wrap it about what transpired subsequently to the other events noticed, we find that it sets, like a garment made by a master hand, upon *Odoacer*, who invaded Italy, smote the Western Empire, represented by the "sun;" conquered Italy, denoted by the "moon," to which this Empire was now practically reduced; and overshadowed the less lights, or rulers, called the "stars"—the senators and consuls and magistrates, who were permitted still to exercise their offices, subject to Odoacer, who was King. For the first time in history, a barbarian was sovereign of Rome; and with his virtual accession to the throne, A. D. 476, passed away forever the Roman Empire in the west. You will see, therefore, that this symbol was not mere guess work; but distinct, as was each of the others, it finds its counterpart in actual fact, the trumpet of Revelation and of the barbarians harmonizing.

There is an interruption now in the sounding of the trumpets, which marks a division. You will understand the first division—the four events, or series of events which contributed so greatly to the downfall of the Roman Empire, which brought about the complete and final overthrow of that Empire in the west. A period of a hundred years follows with events no different in their general meaning from those considered. History turns our eyes now to the east, to Constantinople, which after the final overthrow of the Empire in the west assumed the rights and power of its former rival. It became the seat of the most marked events, which followed thereafter for some centuries; and we shall find that Revelation has next to do with this, as it naturally would from the order of historic events.

Says the apostle, "And I heard and beheld an angel flying (as an eagle) through the midst of heaven, saying with a loud voice, woe, woe, woe, to the inhabitants of the earth, by reason of the other voices of the trumpet of the three angels which are yet to sound." These three trumpets are called the "Woe Trumpets," and the natural inference from this distinction is that they referred to things entirely separate from those which had preceded, and distinct from each other, and greater than any which had gone before.

Listen then, to the sounding of the *fifth* trumpet,—or the first woe trumpet.—Read the representation in chapter 9: 1–11.

The symbol presents one who claims or seems to have come from heaven, but really has the key of the bottomless pit; who shows that he is not from heaven, by unloosing the forces of darkness and evil upon the world. He is evidently the same as the "King over them," and was actuated by the spirit of "the angel of the bottomless pit, whose name in the Hebrew tongue is Abaddon, but in the Greek tongue hath his name Apollyon," or destroyer. The locusts were peculiar to Arabia. The symbol is, therefore, eastern. They were to have power to injure, but they were not to hurt, as was the wont of locusts, "the grass of the earth," "anything green, neither any tree." Their mission of harm was to be aimed at those who were not looked upon as the sealed servants of God. They were not to kill the latter, but should torment them for a definite period; and their oppressions should be of a nature to lead men to desire to die, rather than live amid such circumstances. The locusts were to look like horses, a resemblance which, on a minor scale, has been often remarked in eastern countries. They were to be prepared for battle; so exhibiting in symbol an army of horsemen. The riders had on their heads, as it were, crowns of gold; and "their faces were as the faces of men. And they had hair as the hair of women, and their teeth were as the teeth of lions, and they had breastplates as it were breastplates of iron."

Turning our eyes eastward, do we behold anything of which the Fifth Trumpet was a herald? Looking to the very Arabia whence came locusts, did any person or army spring forth to answer to the sound of this Trumpet of Revelation? In the year 609 A. D., one of the most remarkable men in all the history of the world began to preach, not the gospel of Christ, but himself. He proclaimed, in the year 612, that he came from heaven; but afterward gave evidence that he was allied to the angel of the bottomless pit. He opened this, as it were, and forth issued what darkened the world—a mighty army to be ruled by their king, and to follow him and his successors wherever led: I refer to *Mohammed*, and the *Saracens*.

The number of his hosts could not have been likened to anything better than a cloud of locusts. They were to be commanded not to destroy the grass of the earth, nor any green thing, nor the trees; and in the Koran is found the command: "Let not the victory be stained with the blood of women or children. Destroy no palm trees, nor burn any fields of corn. Cut down no fruit trees, nor do any mischief to cattle, only such as you kill to eat." This was remarkable, according to the usual course of such a people. But they should seek to injure those who had not the seal of God in their foreheads; and it is a fact that Mohammed set out first to destroy idolaters, and then all infidels—all those who did not worship according to the views of his people. But they were not to kill God's servants, though they should torment these. The irritation of their sway should be such as to lead men to prefer death to life. All these things serve to place the symbol aright.

In the *appearance* of the things symbolized do we find additional evidence. They had on their heads, not crowns of gold, but, "as it were" such—what resembled these, as did the yellow turbans of the Saracens. Their faces were man-like, bearded, and not smooth-shaven, as were those of the Goths. Their hair was long like that of women, which was true of the followers of Mohammed; all giving them a savage, and lion-like appearance. They wore breast-plates of iron, answering to the symbol. The rest of the description refers to the wounding, but not fatal, power they should exert.

There is another thing by which the symbol is verified, the *time* the persons symbolized were to torment men. This was to be "five months." In the scripture the term "day" is, prophetically, a year. This use is found in the book of Daniel, and thus the date of Christ's death was prophecied of. That it is so used in the book of Revelation is learned from the saying of Christ to the church at Smyrna: "Ye shall have tribulation ten days," this, doubtless, meaning the Diocletian persecution which prevailed ten years. A prophetic month would be thirty years, and a prophetic year, three hundred and sixty years—a year for a day. Five months would be five times thirty years, or one hundred and fifty years. The Saracens besides their efforts in the east, and their attempts to capture Constantinople, pressed their conquests through Northern Africa, subduing all this country, and passing the straits of Gibraltar, conquered Spain, and marched upward into France. Says Mr. Gibbon: "One hundred years after his (Mohammed's) flight from Mecca, the arms and reigns of his successors extended from India to the Atlantic Ocean, over the various and distant provinces, which may be comprised under the names of Persia, Syria, Egypt, Africa, and Spain." The fate of Christendom was at issue. It was the intention of the Saracens to meet from east and west in Europe, and the world would have been under the dominion of the crescent rather than of the cross. It seemed as if nothing could stop their progress, and it is a matter of surprise to historians that the tide was checked and rolled back. But Charles Martel met the advancing hosts, and dealt a blow which made the invaders recoil; and not many years afterward, their power had greatly waned. Of their own accord, they exchanged their warlike efforts for the pursuits of peace; the arts and sciences, and literature, claiming their attention. Perhaps, the best and most distinct mark of this was the building of Bagdad, the "city of peace," as the capital of the Saracenic Empire, by the Caliph Almanzor, in the year 762. This became the center of the wealth and learning and power of the people. Reckoning from the time Mohammed published the Koran, A. D. 612, to the building of Bagdad, we have one hundred and fifty years, the time sought for the fulfillment of the symbol: all, uniting in showing that the rise and progress of the Saracenic power respond truly to the heraldings of the Fifth Trumpet.

Listen now to the sounding of one other of the trumpets, the *sixth* Trumpet. Read Rev. 9: 13-19.

The location here is definite, the great river Euphrates. The number of the army is given as large, to be reckoned by "myriads," a peculiar term in the original. The horsemen had "breastplates of fire, and of jacinth, and of brimstone;" so, appearing clothed in red, in blue, and in yellow. Fire and smoke and brimstone, seemed to issue out of the mouths of the horses, whose heads appeared like the heads of lions. They who were killed, were "killed by the fire and by the smoke and by the brimstone"—by these united. The horses had not only power in their mouths, but in their tails; "for their tails were like unto serpents, and had heads, and with them they do hurt."

We turn the pages of history for the next important event, or series of events, bearing upon what remained of the old Roman Empire, the Empire of the East, with Constantinople as its capital. What do we find? We look to the river Euphrates named in the symbol, and we behold the rise of a new power; of a power destined to spread far and to last long; one which did, next in order of time, have the most important bearing upon the history of the world—that of the *Turks or Turkmans*.

"Four angels," or "four" powers, are spoken of; and we find that four were connected—the original power which had established itself in Persia, and three which sprang from it—Kerman, Syria, and Roum. These were united just then, a thing which never before occurred, and which never afterward took place in that principality. These were prepared by conquests to the east of the Euphrates, and had been there kept until the time before us. The army was to be an army of "horsemen." The "horses" were seen in the vision, a predominance of cavalry being thus declared; a thing truer of the Turkish forces than of any other army of invaders known in history. Gibbon writes that, "The myriads of Turkish horse overspread a frontier of six hundred miles, from Taurus to Arzeroum." Again speaking of the advance of the Turks, under Togrul, he says: "He passed the Euphrates at the head of the Turkish cavalry." The appearance of the horsemen was that of men having burnished breastplates, or clothing of red, of the color of jacinth, and brimstone—purplish-blue and yellow. As a fact, "From their first appearance, the Ottomans affected to wear warlike apparel of scarlet, blue, and yellow; a descriptive trait the more marked from its contrast to the military appearance of the Greeks, Franks, or Saracens, contemporarily."

From the mouths of the horses "issued fire and smoke and brimstone," and with these they "killed." If such a thing were true in those days that firearms were used; if the horsemen were armed with horse-pistols or the like, we should readily see the force of the symbol: a company of cavalry charging, and blazing with their firearms would answer to the picture. But was there any such thing then? There was, the Turks being among the very first to use firearms, and did use these effectively. But how about their power being in the "tails" of the horses? How is it that with these they should hurt? It is true that the standard of the Turks was at times a horse's tail, or three of these raised upon a spear. But the symbol finds a better and simpler explanation. If the Turks used not only firearms, but artillery; then we could see in batteries hurried along by the fleetness of the horse, whirled about, and discharged, what answers to the description. But were cannon used by the Turks? They were; indeed, the peculiar form of their cannon would be known now as the "basilisk," which means *serpent*.

There remains but one more important question in relation to the symbol of this Trumpet; and that is, the question of *time*. There is a period stated, in which they should continue their career of conquest and war. It is given as "an hour, and a day, and a month, and a year." Reckoning in prophetic time we have 360 + 30 + 1 + 1 hour = 391 + 15. According to the Julian year, it would be 365 + 30 + 1 + 106 days = 396 yrs. + 106 days, Computing from the time that Togrul set forth from Bagdad with his Turkmans, the year 1057 A. D., we arrive at the following: 1057 + (396 years + 106 days) = 1453. If, however, as I believe, to be the uniform prophetic calculation, the year stands for 360 prophetic days; then, counting from the time the Turks commenced their slaughter of Christians, we must date from 1062, when they slew 70,000 of these in Palestine. Thus, we have 1062 + 391 = 1453, the same result being reached as in the other computation, and bringing us to the year in which the Turks captured *Constantinople*, and forever overthrew what remained of the Roman Empire; which, according to the interpretation of the historic symbols thus far, would naturally be embraced.

Taking all together, we arrive at a most startling—from a human stand-point—conformity between the symbol and thing symbolized, an agreement which affords additional evidence of the divine inspiration of the Bible.

Even that which follows; the fact, that notwithstanding all these judgments, all this suffering—in that period when the Turks triumphed over Crusaders seeking to regain Jerusalem, and which ended in the capture of Constantinople by the Ottomans who had early embraced the religion of Mohammed —idolatry, in the professed Christian world continued, together with murders and sorceries, and fornication and thefts; which things, as we shall have occasion to consider more particularly as we progress in our lectures, were practiced and sanctioned in a church which claimed to be Christian, and to be the universal church of Christ.

As the "spectre of Brocken," seen on the summits of the distant hills by the traveller who may stand at sunrise on the topmost ridge of one of the mountains of Germany, is but the shadow of his own form projected upon the mists by the morning sunlight; so, these symbols give the very outlines of the events viewed, moving and changing with these.

The end of the sounding of the Sixth Trumpet brings us, in the scripture itself, not only again to the lesson of faith in the word of God; but to the teaching, that despite judgments and sore disasters, men will go on in their sins, will not repent of their evils. Like those who amid the awful visitations of earthquakes, as eye witnesses have declared, are bent upon plunder and self-gain, unheeding the wrecks of homes and the desolations of life; so will men be regardless of the hand of God in the great events of history, and continue in sin and impenitence. It was so then, it is so now; judgments do not convert the world or the heart, else some of you would have been converted who are yet in your sins. Oh! you need God's spirit, and you need to look to the cross of Christ, to be saved. God grant that you may; that the study of his word, the lessons of his truth, the evidence of the fidelity of this, may be sanctified to your repentance and everlasting salvation, to the praise of his glory.

V.

The Mighty Angel and the Seventh Trumpet.

Revelation, Chapters 10, 11 : 1–18.

OUR last lecture brought us, in order of time, to the middle of the fifteenth century, to the fall of Constantinople, in the year 1453. Notwithstanding the sore judgments which had been inflicted on the world, a period of corruption continued, as declared in the last two verses of the ninth chapter of Revelation, and as is abundantly verified by the history of those times. That century, despite things which were to have a most marked bearing upon the future of mankind; viz, the invention of the art of printing and the discovery of the new world, closed in profound darkness, amid which the sixteenth opened.

If, as I have no doubt, the symbols thus far have truthfully applied to the history of the world, more particularly to that of the Roman

Empire; and if the seven sealed scrolls and the seven sounding trumpets, set forth the secular history of the race, from the time when John wrote the wondrous visions given him by the Lord Jesus, to the end of the world, as is very evident; then, we would naturally look for the realization of the symbols between the sixth and seventh Trumpets, in what followed, in order of time, the events indicated by the former of these.

It would seem as if the power which triumphed so signally in the capture of Constantinople, that of the Turks, was to continue in some form after the sixth Trumpet was sounded. Such we find to be the case, the Ottomans still holding Constantinople and a part of the territory acquired four hundred years ago.

John next saw in vision "*a mighty angel* come down from heaven, clothed with a cloud; and a rainbow was upon his head, and his face was as it were the sun, and his feet as pillars of fire."

This would naturally, if the historic chronology were kept up, have reference to the next great event in history, or be connected with this, if it did not stand for that event itself. We are brought, as I have said, to the sixteenth century. If any thing took place in this which could have an unusual representation, to the accomplishment of which a "mighty angel," mightier than any heretofore introduced, were necessary; then we might hope for a solution of the symbol: for we are yet dealing with symbols, the peculiar language—from first to last—of the book of Revelation. We have been directed in other connections to visions of "stars" which seemed to descend from heaven but really were moved by satanic power, by influences from the bottomless pit. We have seen angels, in vision, coming from parts of the earth, messengers of the divine will; but here we are granted the view of an angel, a "mighty angel" from *heaven*. That angel might personify a great event, serving a purpose heavenly in its origin, and heavenly in its mission and end; or it could set forth some eminently great man, a mighty power among men, sent of heaven, so far as a man could be, for a blessed work; or it may be that the mighty angel was the Lord Jesus Christ, who in other parts of the Bible is so spoken of, and, properly, because he was "the messenger of the covenant." If the latter is the intent, then he would be manifest as coming at that time in an unusual manner, and for a special and good purpose, to do in this way what he had not accomplished by means of his judgments; for, despite these, men repented not of their idolatries, and fornications, and thefts, and murders. I think that the last was intended, that the vision of the angel is a representation of Christ appearing in his providence, subsequent to the fall of Constantinople, while yet the period of impenitence and evil doing was in progress.

We look, then, to the the history of the sixteenth century, that we may find, if possible, any event which would justify such a view; the appearance of any person through whom Christ may be said to have worked in a special manner. We search not in vain; for almost next to the introduction of Christianity into the world and to the final consummation of things, stand, in importance, the events of the sixteenth century. No century, save the early christian age, has, thus far, had more to do with the world's good, its moral welfare, than the sixteenth; and the event which marks this as of so great moment, is, *The Great Reformation.*

Some have likened the event itself to the mighty angel seen in Revelation. The angel may have been intended for the great character, whose name is associated with its beginning and its progress; to wit, Martin Luther. But it is more in consonance with the scripture, and with all the features of even this particular vision, to recognize in the angel the Lord Jesus Christ himself. There are points of resemblance between the view here and the representation of him at the outset of all these revelations. His feet and countenance are seen, here as there, burning with fire and shining as the sun; but now he appears "clothed with a cloud," the emblem of mystery, of glory, of blessing; and with his brow encircled "with a rainbow," the sign of hope, and peace, and covenant faithfulness. He comes to dissipate the moral darkness of the world with the sunlight of his countenance; to move among men as a refiner's fire, to "move in a mysterious way, his wonders to perform;" while above all his doings, and mingling with the brightness of his countenance, are the colors of hope for a storm tossed world, a world deluged with iniquity and practical unbelief—real unbelief of "the truth as it is in Jesus."

The "angel *had in his hand a little book open.*" The word book, as here used, is found nowhere else in the New Testament; usually the word is βιβλίον, but here it is βιβλαρίδιον. The word denotes a little roll or volume. It was a "little book," it was "open," and it was held by an angel, the angel Christ, and, so, for a good purpose. The book might have been, as some have thought, the remaining part of the scroll sealed by the seventh seal; but the peculiarity of the term points to some other book: and, when we take into account that at the time evidently contemplated by the symbol a special book was anew brought to the world, we shall have no difficulty in understanding what the book was— "little," yet what a mighty part to have in the revolution and reformation of the moral world; so little that each person might possess it, and all might read it; so little that we may carry it about with us always, if we will: yet under God the great lever that moves the heart and life, that can move the world—*the Bible.* It was the mainspring of the Reformation, the very first thing which called this forth. When Luther found the Bible on the shelves of the University at Erfurt, he came into the presence of the angel of the Reformation. It was exalted by this, and was and is, as has been declared, "the religion of the Protestants." It had been a sealed book, inaccessible to the people, because of ignorance, on account of the opposition of the papal power to its use by the common people, and inasmuch as it had cost a fortune to purchase this or any other book. But now it was to be an "open" book. An Open Bible, was the plea of the Reformers; and the printing press, lately invented, was to send it forth freely; and to bring it to the hands of the masses of the people, as from the Lord Jesus Christ.

On "sea and land" did the angel set his feet; as denoting not only the rightful possession of these, as being Lord of the whole earth, but as showing that the triumphs of the Reformation were to extend to the islands of the sea, and to the lands beyond the sea, as truly as to that part of the world then considered most important. I believe this to be a plain reference to the conquests of the gospel beyond the sea—but recently crossed—in the New

World, but just discovered. Such a representation could never have been associated so appropriately with any period as with just that time, when voyagers were pushing their discoveries in the new Continent, the outer doors of which had been opened by the hand of Columbus. History shows that in one century after the Reformation began, the principles of this were established, under the Puritans, on these western shores; and they have here gained some of their most glorious successes.

The "angel cried as with a loud voice, as when a lion roareth; and when he had cried seven thunders uttered their voices." So did Luther lift up his voice with the boldness of the lion, and though every tile on all the houses at Worms were a devil, he would yet go to the place to maintain the truth of God's word. The thunders which responded may have been the thunders of the papal "bulls," which were issued against Luther from the seven-hilled city of Rome, which made them seem as seven thunders. If so, it was only a "bull" against a "lion," the papal bull against the "lion of the tribe of Judah," and the latter should not be intimidated. What the voices of the thunders said was not permitted to be written; perhaps, because of no consequence. If, however, the seven thunders were the great responses which history was to make to the Reformation, then, the mystery of their utterances would be a reason for the sealing of these. This, however, is the less probable explanation, as this response is further along brought, in another form, into view. The first is the truer significance.

"And the angel which I saw stand upon the sea, and upon the earth, lifted up his hand to heaven, and swore by him that liveth forever and ever, who created heaven and the things that therein are, and the earth, and the things that therein are, and the sea, and the things which are therein, that there should be time no longer: But in the days of the voice of the seventh angel, when he shall begin to sound, the mystery of God should be finished, as he has declared to his servants the prophets." The oath is in his name who, living forever, can speak of the future as of the present; and who, because he made all things, has the authority and power to declare as to future time. The translation does not give the true sense. The declaration is not that there should be "time no longer;" that is, that there should be no more time, this to come to an end; but that the "*time should not be yet.*" You will see the force of this from the connection. He declared that the "time should not be yet;" "*but in the days of the voice of the seventh angel, when he shall begin to sound, the mystery of God should be finished, as he has declared to his servants the prophets.*" What this "mystery" is which should be finished when the seventh angel begins to sound, you will learn from the 5th verse of the 17th chapter of the book; where we read: "And upon her forehead was a name written, *mystery;*" also, from Daniel 7th chapter, 26th verse: "But the judgment shall sit, and they shall take away his dominion, to consume and destroy it unto the end." There must have been something special to call forth the oath of the angel at this time. It has been thought that it was intended to meet and correct a general and strong expectation which would be then cherished, that the world was soon to come to an end. Such an anticipation did then prevail, and has been strongly felt at other times. John Wickliffe, the Lollards, the Hussites, held to it; Reformed churches and the New England Puritans believed it; and in our own day it has spread as a mighty faith over the world, and even now there are many in this and other lands who look for the speedy personal coming of Christ, and the end of the world. Luther himself expressed a fervent belief in the near advent of Christ. To this Melancthon clung, and Latimer said: "The day is not far off." To correct this—if this were the reference—the angel Christ would affirm with an oath, that the "time is not yet." As he gave all the symbols of the book to the apostle and the early church, to lead them to look forward in patience and faith, to the consummation of his plans in the long future; so, at this period, which was almost next, in order of importance, to the introduction of Christianity upon earth, he would say to his servants, "the time is not yet." *But the special thing*, the time for the end of which was not yet, was "the *mystery of God*, as he has declared to his servants the prophets"—to Daniel especially. With this mystery, and the end of it, we shall have more to do, as we go forward with this and other lectures. The Reformers—Luther and others, thought the papacy was to come to an end in their time. Well might Luther have so judged, since, as a writer then said: "In the space of a fortnight (after he first promulgated his doctrines) they spread over Germany; and within a month they had run through all Christendom; as if angels themselves had been the bearers of them to all men." But the "time was not yet" for its downfall, as we now see to have been true.

"And the voice which I heard from heaven, spake unto me again, and said, Go, and take the little book which is open in the hand of the angel which standeth upon the sea and upon the earth. And I went unto the angel, and said unto him, Give me the little book. And he said unto me, Take it and eat it up; and it shall make thy belly bitter, but it shall be in thy mouth sweet as honey. And I took the little book out of the angel's hand, and ate it up; and it was in my mouth sweet as honey: and as soon as I had eaten it my belly was bitter. And he said unto me, Thou must prophesy again before many peoples, and nations, and tongues, and kings." The little book again comes into prominence, and now was shown how it should perform its mission in the reformation and salvation of the world. It was to be *eaten;* not literally, but mentally, spiritually, as we now speak of devouring the contents of a book. Hence we read of the prophet Ezekiel eating the roll with God's word on it; and Jeremiah said: "Thy words were found, and I did eat them; and thy word was unto me the joy and rejoicing of my heart." The Bible was to accomplish its great purpose by being taken into the mind and soul, as food into the body—masticated and digested, and assimilated to the soul, through the processes of our mental and moral natures, and under the power and blessing of the Holy Spirit. Thus was it welcomed then. With what eagerness was it read and studied! it came to a hungry world; and was heartily, greedily, thankfully, received. The world had long been fed on husks, fit only for swine; it was now to be nourished with the bread of eternal life. As was true of Ezekiel, so of John—as personifying Luther—the contents of the book was as sweet as honey in his mouth; and they both could say with David: "How sweet are thy words unto my taste; sweeter than honey to my mouth." But it was bitter in the consequences it brought to the bodies of God's people; for to read, even to possess it, came to be considered a sufficient reason for the punishment and putting to death of the possessors. Being received, it was to lead the people of God to do again what they had done in early Christian times, to "prophesy," or preach the gospel—now as then, or even more fully, "before many peoples," before the masses; and "nations," divided politically; and "tongues," speaking different languages; and "kings," the rulers of the earth. Preaching, which is so common now, was then a thing of disuse. The pure "preaching" of the gospel, which had marked its early years, had given place, in a corrupt church, to the "performance of rites and ceremonies. Genuflexions, crossings, burning of incense, processions, music," were and still are "the characteristic features of all papal churches." The preaching of the gospel had become "foolishness" to them, as it was to the Greeks in the time of the Apostles; but it was still "the power of God unto salvation." But it was *Bible* preaching, the proclamation of the truth as it is in Jesus, as this was taken from his word, which moved the hearts of men; not that of worldly wisdom; not that preaching where enough of the Bible is worked in among nice sayings and learned words to redeem it utterly from the wisdom of man's speech, enough to give it a coating of the gospel. The Bible was not made the clothing and ornament of the gospel, but it was the body of this; and whatever else was used only covered this, not to conceal, but, as in all true adornment, to set forth the substance.

Now follows, still in connection with the great vision before us—of the Reformation, a *measurement of the temple*, or true church of God; temple standing for church. "There was given me a reed like unto a rod"—it was given to John as if he lived at the time of the fulfillment of the symbol, or, as if he prophetically used it; and the word was: "Rise and measure the temple of God, and the altar, and them that worship therein." A standard by which these were to be determined was placed in his hand, which, doubtless, was the word of God, here spoken of in another form, and by which the lives of professed Christians were to be tested. He was to declare what constituted the true church of Christ, what was the true altar, and who the true members of the church. A distinction was to be made between these and all other things; and the latter were to be "left out," or "cast out," as not true.

These were themes of vital moment then, when there was a professed church which claimed to be the only true church; when the way of salvation was connected with church "altars," and sacrifice was supposed to be made through the "mass;" when a Romish priesthood had taken the place of gospel preachers; and when, as it were, the "court of the Gentiles" should be full of those who appeared to be members of the temple, but who were only seemingly connected with this. As a matter of fact, these were the great questions which were brought forth in the Reformation; a measurement of the things specified was made. "What is the church?" "How shall man be just with God?" "Who are his true people?"—were most common, as they were important inquiries brought before the people. Luther and the Reformers took ground against the claims and teachings of the papacy; holding, in particular, that we are saved only by faith in Jesus, and not by good works; and that experimental religion is alone true. But nominal Christians should still exist as in the court of the Gentiles, and they should "tread the holy city"—which Rome had come to be regarded, "under foot, forty and two months," or 1260 years.

During this time which is again mentioned in another form, as one thousand two hundred and three score days, "witnesses" should continue to prophesy in that city, "clothed," however, "in sackcloth," or in mourning, in sadness and in distress. The number "two" is the scripture number for *competent*. The truth was to be established by two witnesses. These may be those, who in the east and west, testified for Christ and the truth, during the long rule of the papal power; and who should continue to do so, even though "clothed in sackcloth." They were the remaining "candlesticks" or churches—so, in reality, even if they had no name; and may have been the Paulicians in the east and Waldenses in the west, who really began their history about the same year, and near the time when the papal power commenced to assume its fearful position. Their fire should be kept alive by oil from the two olive trees, or preachers who should minister by their words to the life of the true churches of Christ. However man might regard them, they "stood before the God of the earth;" and were not lost sight of by him, but were his witnesses, and should not be wholly destroyed.

Seemingly, and outwardly, they might be; but the fire from their mouth, their burning words of truth, should devour the pretensions of their enemies; and the fulfillment of that truth should be the destruction of these. As God had said to Jeremiah, so did the Lord say to these witnesses: "Because ye speak this word, behold I will make my words in thy mouth fire, and this people wood, and it shall devour them." "In this manner," they should be "killed;" not by material power wielded by the witnesses or churches; but by the power of truth, belching like fire from their mouth. With the opposition to these should be connected the ills, the famines, the wars, the plagues, which came upon the earth, in the days of their prophecy. God answered their prayers for deliverance from their enemies, for triumph, in his own way; and while he brought forth the fire, he, also, visited the people with his judgments: yet "repented they not." So that, what we saw, in our last lecture, come upon the world, is here explained as being in judgment for the persecutions visited upon the true people of God.

When the time of the completion of the testimony

of the first long series of witnesses should come, "the beast that ascended out of the bottomless pit" —it was said—"shall make war against them, and shall overcome them and kill them." The beast is afterward more particulary noticed, but his origin is here stated. Like Mohammed, like the Mohammedan religion and power, it is said to have come from "the bottomless pit;" from beneath, not above; from hell, not from heaven. It was not a mere persecution, but a "war" that should be waged. The war against the Waldenses is in point; that war forming in its record "one of the darkest pages of history," when whole villages were swept away, every inhabitant, in some instances, being slaughtered; and which extended from 1540–1570, no less than 900,000 Protestants being put to death. A crusade was proclaimed by the Pope against the true people of God, whom he was pleased to call "heretics." To all of which may be added the horrors of the Inquisition, which warred against the saints; the wars of Philip II., aimed at these; the 50,000,000 persons slain—from first to last—by the papal power, on account of religion.

Amid the 1260 years there was to be a time when

it appeared to the world as if the witnesses were dead. They had served the will of God, and their enemies seemed to have triumphed over them; and their dead bodies lay "in the great city, which spiritually is called Sodom and Egypt," because of its evils and the hard bondage it inflicted, and which —spiritually—is "where, also, our (or their) Lord was crucified"—as if crucified afresh in their death. As unburied, were they to be pointed at in their death, to be viewed in the great city. A gathering from the people, or "they of the people, and kindreds, and tongues, and nations," should look upon their dead bodies for a definite time—"three days and a half;" and not suffering their bodies to be buried, they would rejoice over these, and "make merry and send gifts one to another, because these two prophets tormented them that dwelt on the earth"—tormented their consciences through preaching the truth. "And after three days and a half the spirit of life from God entered into them, and they stood upon their feet." Searching for a time when the "two witnesses" seemed to be wholly overcome, when a gathering of people looked as upon their dead bodies in the great city, we find that at the beginning of the 16th century the papal power was dominant. A writer says that, "Everything was quiet; every heretic was exterminated, and the whole christian world supinely acquiesced in the enormous absurdities inculcated by the Romish church." But, a very definite time is set when this state of things should be viewed by an assemblage of people. In the year 1513 a celebrated council was held at Rome, the council of Lateran, so called because held in a palace thus named. To this all dissentients were summoned, but none whatever appeared. During the sessions of the council, the orator of the session entered the pulpit, and amid great applause, said what was never said before and never could be said again: 'There is an end of resistance to the papal rule and religion; opposers there exist no more;' and, 'The whole body of christendom is now seen to be subjected to its head, the pope.' That council closed 'in the splendor of the dinners and fêtes given by the cardinals.' 'The assembled princes and prelates separated from the council with complacency, confidence, and mutual congratulations on the peace, unity, and purity of the church.' The dead bodies were thus viewed by the assemblage from the "people, kindreds, and tongues, and nations," for the council represented the entire Roman power; and there was "merry making" over the death of the witnesses. The remarkable words proclaiming this were used May 5th, 1514. Three days and a half, prophetically, from this time, "the spirit of life from God" should again enter into the witnesses. This time would be 3 years + 180 days. This would give us as follows: Three years, May 5th, 1517. Including the 5th we should have, for May, 27 days; June, 30; July, 31; August, 31; September, 30; and October, 31, = 180. To October 31st, 1517, we would obtain the three years and a half, *the year and day on which Luther nailed his celebrated Theses to the doors of the church at Wittemberg;* the day when "the spirit of life from God" entered anew his witnesses, and the day when the Reformation began: a most remarkable fulfillment of the word of God, of even the symbols of this.

The *effect* was startling. "Great fear fell upon them which saw them." The witnesses were exalted as to heaven, "and their enemies saw them" so glorified; which was true of the Reformers, who became objects of universal attention, even Henry

VIII. of England aiming darts at Luther, and gaining from the Pope the name of "Defender of the Faith." "In that same hour was there a great earthquake," a great commotion and overturning among the nations, among those heretofore subject to the great city; which every reader of history knows to have taken place, at least a "tenth part" of its dominion falling away: an earthquake, a commotion, attended with the slaying of thousands. Germany, Switzerland, Denmark and Sweden, were soon, in good part, turned from Rome, and England became nominally Protestant; and "the remnant were affrighted, and gave glory to the God of heaven."

One thing remains concerning this part of the Revelation, the *time* of the power of those who should tread under foot the holy city, and during which the witnesses there should prophesy in sackcloth. The time is given as forty-two months, or one thousand two hundred and three score days. This same power is spoken of as the "mystery of God," and it does seem a mystery that God should have allowed it to exist; and it is said that the end of it had been "declared to his servants the prophets." In the 7th chapter of Daniel, the same power is prophesied of, and the same time is set forth, as "a time and times and the dividing of time;" that is, a year, two years, and one-half of a year, which prophetically would be 360 + 720 + 180 = 1260 years. In Daniel it is plainly revealed that the object assumed civil authority, and grew out of the "fourth beast," or Roman power; thus giving us the *papal civil power*. To estimate the duration of this we should need to know just when this arose, which is one of the most difficult questions of history, since that power as such grew so gradually. But there are several events which help us in this, and I am able to point you to what I believe to be a correct verification of the time. In the year 606, A. D., Pope Boniface sought recognition as Universal Bishop from the Emperor Phocas. Whether it was directly granted or not, as has been questioned, here was a positive effort to grasp power; and this time dates the "Papacy." Dr. Schaff says: "The Roman bishops called themselves not patriarchs, but popes, that they might rise the sooner above their colleagues; for the one denotes oligarchical power, and the other, monarchical." This claim is represented as reaching its height in the latter part of the sixth century. Leo I. sought earlier than this an alliance, defensive and offensive, of the spiritual and the temporal powers, "in the pursuit of an unlimited sovereignty." With the final dissolution of the Roman Empire, the papal power, "to a certain extent, stepped into the imperial vacancy, and the successors of Peter became in the mind of the Western nations, sole heir of the old Roman imperial succession." "With Gregory I., 590–604, a new period begins." "He marks the transition of the patriarchal system *into the strict* papacy of the middle ages." We are justified, then, in the belief that the ruling power of the popes virtually commenced in the year 606, from which time they called themselves Universal Bishops. If we are to date from the actual possession of kingly power by these, then we must look to the year when the exarchate of Ravenna—the sovereignty of this and of Rome, was granted to the Pope by Pepin, King of France, A. D., 752. Dating from the latter, we have $752 + 1260 = 2012$; from the former, $606 + 1260 = 1866$.

I know that the civil power of Rome has been repeatedly prostrated—even as late as 1848, and has anew arisen; and when I speak of the things which have again wrested the crown from the pope, I am aware that there is doubt as to the year, when it was first worn, and that the authority may be again gained. But there is far less likelihood of it now than heretofore, and there is a combination of circumstances which would lead us to believe that the end has come which the prophets foretold, and which Christ pictured in the revelation he gave. A few years ago, a war occurred in Europe which had direct bearing upon the papal power. Austria, the chief friend and support of Rome, armed against Prussia, the German Confederation and Italy. In one of the shortest campaigns of history the issue was decided; Austria was smitten down, and Victor Emanuel became possessor of Venitia, and moved in purpose toward Rome. The battle of Sadowa decided the fate of Rome, and that was fought—as the whole campaign took place—in the year 1866. Only one power remained to support the papacy, and that was soon crippled and humiliated; in five years, it, also, fell, and with its fall actually took place the downfall of the temporal power of the Pope, Rome passing into the hands of the Italian government. Because of these things am I led to believe that now—in our day, has the scripture been fulfilled; and that as we listen intently, we may hear,

The Sounding of the *Seventh* Trumpet.

The great woe of the sixth Trumpet fell upon the world through the Turkmans; and upon the papal power and the earth through the "earthquake" which attended the exaltation of the witnesses. Not the work of the "mighty angel" of the Reformation produced the woe; any more than the sounding of the seventh or third woe trumpet, shall, in its moral aspects be calamitous, for these are declared to be most glorious: in the one case as in the other, the disaster is to the enemies of God.

At the beginning—when the trumpet "begins to sound," the "mystery," it was declared, shall be finished; the mystery of the duration of the temporal power of Rome, prophesied of by Daniel and foretold by the Lord Jesus. Not that the spiritual power should then end, or has ended; for we read, Daniel 7 : 26, "But the judgment *shall sit*, and they shall take away his dominion, to consume and destroy it *unto the end*," which makes manifest a *gradual* doing away of the Ecclesiastical power, which is to be overcome, as you will see by the connection in Daniel, by the saints: "*They* shall take away his dominion."

I shall not dwell upon the sounding of the seventh Trumpet. I do not need to: for there is given here only a brief summary of that, which, as the thread of history is anew taken up in more purely Ecclesiastical relations, is brought forth more fully as we again approach the end. But the grand result is, evidently, to grow out of the Reformation, from those principles which then sprang up and have remained at work in the world.

Suffice it, that "the kingdoms of this world" are to become the kingdom of our Lord and of his Christ; that the beginning of this time is now at hand. The sounding of the Seventh Trumpet, like that of the others is not sudden, nor audible to the natural ear, nor does it end with one blast: it covers, we know not, how long; but like some of the others, it may embrace scores and hundreds of years. If, however, the interpretation given be true, then we may date the time when the great principles of Christianity are to go forward to sure and complete victory among the nations. The kingdoms or nations shall remain such, political divisions may continue to separate these; but the principles of justice, of truth, of right, .of peace, are to increase henceforth in their dominion, until all the nations shall be swayed by these. Civil and social and religious oppression and wrong are to cease; all people are to be brought into subjection to the higher laws and precepts of a true Christianity, of the Bible, of our Lord and his Christ.

Then cometh the judgment and "the time of the dead that they should be judged;" then shall be "given reward unto God's servants, the prophets and to the saints, and them that fear his name, both small and great;" then, also, "shall be destroyed them which destroy the earth."

With the 18th verse of the 11th chapter, properly ends the connection; with the 19th verse, a retracing of steps takes place.

I point you, again, to the argument, the evidence in favor of the truthfulness of God's word. We have a cumulative argument, for the evidence piles itself up in favor of the Divine inspiration of the scriptures. Can you resist it? If the Bible is true in these things, is it not equally true in all that it declares about you? concerning your condition as sinners? your need of the Lord Jesus Christ, as your atoning and all-sufficient, and only, and living Savior? Is it not true that you must repent or you shall perish, with all the enemies of our God and of his Christ? that you must believe on the Lord Jesus Christ in your hearts to the saving change of these? and that if you believe not, you shall be lost, shall be "damned?"

O ye people of God, rejoice, for now is your salvation nigher than when you believed. Behold our work now, as victory is promised—to go forth with moral weapons to the conquest and salvation of the world, for our God and his Christ. We are entered upon the last days, the consummation days of history, of all time, of the glorious gospel of the Son of God. Triumphs surpassing those of its early days, and of the Reformation, are before us; unsullied now by the mistakes then made by professed Christians, in making Christianity a temporal power, and in linking together church and state: all the spirit of the time is against these errors, and the true church itself is opposed to them. We are entered upon triumphs which shall not give way to disasters, for our God "shall reign forever and ever."

All heaven rejoices: especially the "four and twenty elders," the representatives of the church in heaven, "which sat before God," do now fall upon their faces and "worship God," saying: "We give thee thanks, O Lord God Almighty, which art, and wast and art to come; because thou hast taken to thee thy great power, and hast reigned."

The dominion of truth has commenced. We, on the earth, thank and worship God for it. Be the heart inspired for the victory to be gained. Press forward the lines of Immanuel! With spiritual weapons let us subdue the world to Christ! Nerve every arm for action; and be it our prayer—

> "Fly abroad thou mighty gospel,
> Win and conquer, never cease;
> Let thy lasting, wide dominion,
> Multiply and still increase."

VI.
The Glorious Woman and Warring Beasts.

Revelation, Chapters 11: 19.   12, 13.

THERE is in the portion of the book of Revelation which this lecture covers, a grand grouping of visions, of symbolic representations. It is vastly comprehensive. It goes back, and while the symbols are linked to those we have already viewed, they present most prominently events in *ecclesiastical* history; they have to do with the church peculiarly, with the church true and the church false; with the "woman," the true church of Christ; the "beast," the false church. There is, also, a reaching forward to the ultimate condition of things. We shall find that for the second, out of three times, is the end of all things touched upon, as if the Lord Jesus would keep this before his people for their consolation and support amid all the trials and sufferings of life and of history. The first time, as we saw in our last lecture, the end of all history from a civil or political stand-point was represented, "the kingdoms of this world" becoming "the kingdom of our Lord and his Christ." In the comprehensive summary of the ecclesiastical history of the Christian centuries, which is next given to us, we are taken onward, in thought, to the time when the reapers shall go forth to gather from the professed church of Christ, and from the world, all his true people, according to his own declarations when upon earth; and the angel of justice and destruction shall collect for the wine-press of the wrath of God all that offend in his kingdom. Subsequently, after some more specific representations of things already in part declared, the end of the world, in all its moral bearings, is symbolized. When I say, "end of the world, end of all things," I do not mean that the world is necessarily to be stripped of all people and literally destroyed; but there is to be a close of that order of things which has prevailed from the beginning, an end of the mixed condition of human life and of the forces working upon earth.

I. The time set forth by the first vision pictured in the 12th chapter is, evidently, an early age. This is manifest from a figure, partially the same as that given when first the "door was opened in heaven," and the historic visions were about to commence. Moreover, the symbol of the "dragon" would have force peculiarly in the second and third centuries and onward. It came to be in the second century, more particularly in the third, and for sometime afterward, the Roman ensign, being connected with the "Eagle."

As the "temple of God was opened in heaven, there was seen in his temple the ark of his testament: and there were lightnings, and voices, and thunderings, and an earthquake, and great hail." We see disclosed in the vision the *moral world*, and *the church of Christ*, the repository of the word of God, as the tabernacle and temple contained, within the ark, the tables of the testament inscribed with the law of God. We behold that world at a time when the lightnings were flashing, the thunders were rolling, the voices were speaking, the earthquake was trembling, and the great hail was beating down; which things have already been exhibited in connection with the history of the Roman Empire. The time, withal, is before the commencement of the period of 1260 years which we computed in our last lecture.

Our attention is now especially attracted to the *church of Christ* A "great wonder" or "sign appeared in heaven," in the moral world; "a woman clothed with the sun, and the moon under her feet, and upon her head a crown of twelve stars." This figure of a woman is a familiar embodiment of the church of God in the Bible, and was before this time thus spoken of: "Who is she that looketh forth as the morning, fair as the moon, clear as the sun, and terrible as an army with banners?" She is clothed with the sunlight of truth, and reflects that truth to the world, the reflection being from under her feet and shining as from the twelve apostles, who are as a crown of stars about her brow. As she appears, she is not the infant church; she is a *woman*.

What was then connected with her and what followed, has been explained as portraying the birth of Christ, as the son born unto God's people, the "child" given to the world, on whose "shoulders" should rest "the government," and who was soon caught up to the throne of God, beyond the reach of his enemies that early endeavored to destroy him—that, in the person of Herod, sought the young child, to kill him. If the church could be said to be the mother of Christ, this would be most beautifully and truly represented by the figure before us; but Christ is rather the source of the church, the head and "husband" of this, than the child: and the things seen were to be "hereafter," however soon. I do not say positively that this is not the intent of the figure; only, I think not. This has been interpreted as embodying a time of increase in the church, when this should be multiplied; but this explanation does not so fully answer all the features of the symbol as still another interpretation I give to you.

From all the circumstances, it seems to me that the symbol sets forth the church at a time when there should be earnest, painful cries to *know the truth, to bring forth the word of God.*

There is a two-fold delineation of a long general period, the two features akin as bringing the church of God to that era when this should fly, as a hunted woman, into the wilderness; yet distinctly divided, according to the symbol and as ecclesiastical history displays. The first part appears in the birth of the child, the second in the "war" which took place in the moral world.

The church which cannot be said to be the mother of Christ, can be called the mother of the truth; for it has pleased God to communicate his word to us through inspired servants. The child born of the christian church was the *New Testament of our Lord Jesus Christ*, which came fully to its birth in the production of the Apocalypse: all becoming the object of the special care of divine providence, and being exalted in his kingdom, even "caught up to his throne;" and guarded with peculiar zeal by his people. In this and with this, Christ is seen coming forward in the latter days to rule the world. As early as the second century, the New Testament canon was virtually decided and generally acknowledged. The first great question settled, after the time of the apostles, was: "What writings form the inspired books of the New Testament?" It was a most earnest question; one not decided without travail of soul.

The Adversary stood ready to devour the New Testament, to destroy the truth. His form is that of "a great red dragon, having seven heads and ten horns, and seven crowns upon his heads." This was an outward power through which Satan acted, who is later connected with the dragon; working in this way as he did through the serpent in the garden of Eden. The power was plainly "pagan Rome." The "seven heads are seven mountains," as we find by Revelation 17: 9; the "ten horns" signify ten parts into which the Empire should be divided. At this time the latter were uncrowned, the seven crowns resting on the "heads," or the original seat of government, and denoting the seven forms of government which should there successively prevail: Kings, Consuls, Dictators, Decemvirs, Military Tribunes, Emperors, and Dukes. The dragon appeared in "heaven," as entering the moral world in conflict with the truth.

This period is given a distinct place in church history; and is called by a very eminent church historian—one of the latest and best, Dr. Schaff—the "second period," who places it between A. D. 100–311. It was marked by pagan opposition to the truth of the Bible and of Christianity in general, such men as Tacitus, Celsus and Lucian, leading in that conflict which brought forth, on the part of the church, the early Christian "apologetics." It was, moreover, pre-eminently the age of pagan persecution.

I think that no clearer verification of the symbol could be given than this period affords; its different phases illustrating the efforts to destroy the New Testament truth—the child of the Christian church. While the Truth is involved in the next symbol, that of the "war in heaven," it is not in its birth, but rather in its vindication; that birth taking place as the first century closed and being first disputed, the great war pictured coming afterward. The twelve stars about the head of the woman form an index of the apostolic age of the church—already passed; of the completed labors of the apostles, who are placed as a crown upon her brow, and whose chief work was the production of the New Testament scriptures.

If Mr. Gibbon can be said to have undesignedly furnished a commentary on the symbols which portrayed the civil history of the Roman Empire; so have church historians, without any purpose of so doing, given expression to facts of ecclesiastical history which verify those symbols of Revelation which relate to this.

The next scene is that of a *moral conflict*, the picture of such. "And there was *war in heaven:* Michael and his angels fought against the dragon; and the dragon fought and his angels."

That there was a time which could be so represented, is true. It immediately followed the one just viewed. To it is given the name of an *age*, called the "Patristic age," and designated by Dr. Schaff as the "third period" of church history, extending to the year 600, A. D., and marking the limit of what is called "Ancient Christianity." The conflict could be said, at this period, to have been "in heaven" with more force than at any time before; for it was carried on greatly in the nominal kingdom of God, within the professed churches of Christ, among Christians. Our eyes cannot distinguish fully the lines of battle as God viewed these, nor can we say always which embodied Christ and his people, or Satan and his servants; but of the conflict there is no doubt.

There was questioning and debating—fierce, even dreadful disputes, as to what the word of God taught; concerning its doctrines, among many other things, of the nature of Christ, the divinity of the Holy Spirit, the character of the Trinity, and the form of the church. Councils were held, not necessarily of binding authority, most certainly possessed of no inspired right—for inspiration was limited to the production of the word of God; and, at best, since the days of the apostles, we have had only *illumination*, which is not given peculiarly to ecclesiasticisms, but to the humble, believing, child-like heart, God still revealing the meaning of his word unto "babes." Christian men struggled with the great truths of the Scripture teeming in their minds and souls, and sought to give expression to those truths. To say that they made no mistakes, would be to say that they were infallible, which was not the case. But they certainly announced some doctrines which were like the conclusions of science; that were gathered from the word of God as scientific statements from the realm of nature—statements open to modification, in the one case and the other, as a better, wider, more thorough knowledge of the Bible and of nature, should be gained: for changes of human creeds by no means impair the word of God, no more than does the progress of science affect the material universe; which forever remain, and need to be searched to be known.

Following this conflict, and growing out of it, was the flight of the true church into the wilderness. The Waldenses—known then by another name—resisted the newly acquired authority of the Pope of Rome as soon as this was assumed—in the year 606—and the church in the wilderness retained its belief in the pure truth. One phase of the warfare culminated in the announcement of the doctrine of *"free grace"* by Augustine, which was clung to by Wickliffe, Huss, and Wessel, who looked to his writings next to those of the apostle Paul. Luther was greatly indebted to him; as were, also, Melancthon and Zwingle. Dr. Schaff says: "The Reformers were led by his writings into a deeper understanding of Paul, and so prepared for their great vocation. No church teacher did so much to mould Luther and Calvin; none furnished them so powerful weapons against the dominant Pelagianism and formalism; none is so often quoted by them with esteem and love." "Augustine may be called, in respect of his doctrine of sin and grace, the first forerunner of the Reformation." "Had he lived at the time of the Reformation, he would in all probability have taken the lead of the evangelical movement against the prevailing Pelagianism of the Roman church."

That this conflict was great enough to receive a distinct notice in a revelation portraying prominently the history of the church, is confirmed by the important part "symbolism" has had in the church, in modern as in ancient times,—by the earnest battle still waged over "Confessions of Faith," these standing in the estimation of Christian churches as embodiments of Bible truth.

"That old serpent, called the Devil, and Satan, which deceiveth the whole world, was cast out;" "he was cast out into the earth, and his angels were cast out with him." He went forth, baffled in his other attempts, to work deception in the minds of men as to the truth, and to persecute the true church of Christ. His deceptions have been most woefully carried on; Satan, who was unable to prevent the introduction of Bible-christianity into the world, doing his utmost to delude the nations as to its nature, and spreading his deceptions over the ages and hundreds of millions of people; so that the larger part of professed Christians even to-day are sunken in ignorance and superstition. He betrayed men into linking the idolatry of Paganism and the rites of Judaism with the name of Christianity, into putting out the life and retaining only the dead form of a church.

The truth had been brought forth despite the efforts of Satan, and the triumph was a subject of rejoicing in the "heavens." "A loud voice said, Now is come salvation and strength, and the kingdom of our God, and the power of his Christ: for the accuser of our brethren is cast down, which accused them before our God day and night." The truth was established, and Satan could not buffet the minds of God's people with doubts, as if accusing them "before God night and day." They "overcame him by the blood of the Lamb"—through the virtue of that blood, indeed, but by faith in this; by the great truth of salvation by grace through "the blood of the Lamb;" and by "the word of their testimony," to the power of that grace and blood; and because of this, "they loved not their lives unto the death." Therefore, was the word: "Rejoice ye heavens, and ye that dwell in them;" but it was "woe to the earth," for Satan was to go forth into this, using all his power, for his time was short, or limited.

This time was, also, one of persecution for conscience sake, and dates what are called "Christian persecutions:" these being, rather, unchristian, and instigated by Satan, who impelled even the minds of some good men to it; so manifesting himself still as the great deceiver.

A general description is now given of the exile of the church, during its long period of persecution—"a time, and times, and half a time," $360 + 720 + 180 = 1260$ years. Added to the conflict, many other events conspired to send the true church of Christ into obscurity: the incoming of the Northern barbarians, the uniting of the professed church with the state, and the consequent turning of the minds of many professed Christians from the pure truth of the word of God. Swiftly, as on eagle wings, should she fly into the "wilderness;" but there should she live, for she should be nourished with the truth, and the divine spirit and grace. The dragon sought to destroy the church in the wilderness, by a long continued stream of opposition; but the "earth helped the woman, the earth opened her mouth and swallowed up the flood which the dragon cast out of his mouth;" as if the very conformations of the earth, its opening valleys, were a means of safety to God's people, which we find to have been, in part, the case. These were called the Vaudois, or "people of the valleys;" because they lived in these, here seeking refuge. "Wroth with the woman," the dragon "went to make war with the remnant of her seed" near at hand, which kept "the commandments of God, and have the testimony of Jesus Christ."

There is in all this a pictorial view of the efforts of Satan, who appears as the prime mover, the secret source of the endeavors to injure and destroy the truth and the church; of his workings through pagan Rome, and, in general, through all that has been done, during all the Christian ages, to pervert the truth and to overcome the true disciples of the Lord Jesus Christ.

II. Next appears the symbol of a *"beast"*—savage, brutal, ravenous, blood-thirsty. It is seen rising out of the sea, as out of troublous times; when there was agitation and uncertainty, of which it was born.

A *description* is given of the beast. He had "seven heads and ten horns, and upon his horns ten crowns, and upon his heads the name of blasphemy." You will see that in some respects the beast was like the dragon. The heads were the same, and it had ten horns; but the "crowns" now rested upon the "horns," and upon the heads, instead of the crowns, was the name of "blasphemy." "The seven heads are the seven mountains." Rome stands forth again, but the old power is changed. There are now "ten horns" or kingdoms in the old Roman Empire; this, with its seven crowns, or forms of government, having given way to ten kingdoms, and upon the seven hilled city was a power which was blasphemous,—a power which, in its assumptions could be well named "blasphemy." No truer nor more striking description could be given of the world succeeding the time of pagan Rome than this. The seven hilled city remained; and upon this, was the boasting and self-exalting papal church; while the kingly crowns were distributed among ten governments. Even Romanists admit that the Roman Empire came to be divided into ten kingdoms. These are given by various authors substantially the same; as, the Vandals, in Africa; the Alians, in Spain; Suevi, in Gaul; Heruli, in Italy; Franks, Visigoths, Ostrogoths, Burgundians, Lombards, and Britons. The time of the beast dates from about 600, A. D. the close of the last period we viewed, and when the assumptions of the papacy were fully made.

The beast had a combination of dreadful features. He was "like unto a leopard," distinguished for blood-thirstiness and cruelty, and which was thus the emblem of a power fierce and tyrannical; "his feet were as the feet of a bear," in which lies the strength of the bear; "and his mouth, as the mouth of a lion," with which the lion seizes and holds its prey: thus, the agility and fierceness of the leopard is united with the brutal strength of the bear, and the ravenous, tearing nature of the lion.

The *source* of his power is given. This comes from the same quarter whence the other—the "red dragon," derived his strength; viz., *Satan.* "The dragon gave him his power and his seat, and great authority." We behold a mingling of powers—of the beast and of the ten horns, these working together. The ten horns worshiped the dragon and the beast. They gave power unto the beast to speak great things, and "power was given unto him to continue forty and two months;" or, the 1260 years, which forms so marked a period, in view of the oft repeated use of the term.

"One of the heads" of the old dragon had been wounded to death, and the wound was healed; evidently, by the beast. That head was the "imperial" authority which was healed, or restored, in Charlemagne, by the papal church. The beast became a great wonder; and, seemingly, an invincible power. Dreadful were its blasphemies, really aimed against God, as it blasphemed "his name and his tabernacle" or true church, and "them that dwell therein;" of which papal Rome was guilty. He "made war" with the saints; power was given by the ten horns to do so, and to overcome them, as we saw in our last lecture. "All kindreds, and tongues, and nations," became subject to the beast; kings should hold their crowns at his will, and the nations should own his authority, and all the kindreds bow to him; which came to pass. The whole earth worshiped him, except the true people of God— unwritten and unknown, like the 7,000 faithful ones, in the time of Elijah, who had not bowed their knee to Baal; whose names were known only on high, where they were "written in the book of life of the Lamb slain from the foundation of the world."

Doubtless, the connection of the church of Rome with the temporal powers of the earth, is here set forth—the union of church and state; the one helping the other, which union was to continue 1260 years; the papal power to be upheld during that time, and this, in turn, to sustain kingdoms, at times, to have authority over all these. This power and this alliance maintained by the sword was to perish with the sword, was to be severed by the blows of war; as we see to have been the case, in the gradual weakening and alienation of the nations from Rome, and in the final strokes which have sundered this from the kingdoms of the earth.

I believe that this has been fully accomplished; that, as I showed you, in the last lecture, the 1260 years expired in 1866, or thereabouts; and, with the humbling of Austria and France, and the seizure of Rome by the Italian forces—with the present wresting of the crown from the brow of the Pope, the time set forth in the symbols has been fulfilled. If not, then I am sure that in 138 years from now, it certainly will be; that, the fifth generation from this shall see the final destruction of the temporal authority of the Pope. But I judge from all the evidence, that this has already occurred; that, in view of the symbol of the first beast, and from the identification of the 1260 years with its existence, there can be no question but that the coalition which virtually took place in the year 606 has ended. Thank God, that the date of the decree of papal infallibility marks the downfall of the papal power.

The "Catholic World," in an article just published, says: "By a remarkable coincidence the Franco-Prussian war broke out at the very moment when the dogma of papal infallibility was defined, and immediately after the capitulation of Sedan, Victor Emanuel took possession of Rome. The Pope was without temporal power—a prisoner indeed." So that even Romanists recognize the connection, though blinding their eyes to the meaning of God's providence, which thus annuls that infamous decree; and just when the Pope "exalted himself above all that is called God, or that is worshiped; so that he as God sitteth in the temple of

God, showing himself that he is God," came forth the sentence of downfall burned in letters of fire, and he was made less than the kings of the earth. "History records no more striking example of swift retribution of criminal ambition."

III. "Another beast" now appears. This came from an established order of things, as from "the land" and not from the sea. This is evidently an image of the papal church, in a phase of it which should continue—with another name, it may be—when its temporal power should pass away. The form here brought to view, while connected with the other, and having features in common, may be said to have arisen more especially at the "Council of Trent," at which time church historians place the full rise of "Romanism proper." Then was expressed what had existed and been practiced before, but now came to its full development. It gave "Romanism proper" "symbolical expression and anathematized the doctrines of the Reformation." Moreover, this period marked a renewed and greater grasping for temporal power, on the part of the papal church.

This beast had "two horns like a lamb:" it appeared to be lamb-like, as the papal church has always professed, even when it was speaking like the dragon, like the dragon we have viewed. "He exerciseth all the power of the first beast before him, and causeth the earth and them which dwell therein to worship the first beast, whose deadly wound was healed." That this was carried out by the papal authority is an historic fact; that the power represented by the first beast, was maintained by the ecclesiastical authority of Rome, is true; even now is that power claimed by the Pope and the Romish hierarchy.

A peculiarity of its mode of securing and preserving its authority is given, this being the great wonders he should do—the "lying wonders," the false miracles; so, "deceiving them that dwell on the earth by the means of those miracles he had power to do in the sight of the beast; saying to them that dwell on the earth, that they should make an image to the beast, which had the wound by a sword and did live." Thus has the papal church endeavored to secure submission to its authority, to its temporal as well as ecclesiastical dominion.

"And he had power to give life unto the image of the beast, that the image of the beast should both speak, and cause that as many as would not worship the image of the beast should be killed. And he causeth all, both small and great, rich and poor, free and bond, to receive a mark in their right hand, or in their foreheads : and that no man might buy or sell, save he that had the mark, or the name of the beast, or the number of his name."

To give life "to the image of the beast," was one of the objects of the council of Trent. It was to be done by a vindication of the papal authority in word, which was to be followed by the persuasiveness of the sword. Whatever growing discontent had manifested itself among Catholics or princes, was, by skillful manipulation, rendered nugatory in the council. Not simply old doctrines of the papacy were re-affirmed, but new enormities were produced. The world was made to worship the old beast, unto whose image new life was given; not to own his authority, was at the peril of life. The old did not pass away, but a more solidified ecclesiasticism arose—called forth by the times—to support the former pretensions of the papacy, which were in danger among the nations.

The beast had, in its old form, favored its votaries,

and declared that Catholics should not buy nor sell to those who pretended to interpret the word of God for themselves—the "heretics." The spirit was retained which led the council of Lateran, under Pope Alexander III.; the synod of Tours, under the same Pope; and, also, Pope Martin V., in a bull issued after the council of Constance, to decree that no business dealings should be had with heretics.

But that the question as to what is intended by the beast, might be placed beyond doubt, its name is given in a way more familiar in early times than now—in the form of a *number*. It was written in the Greek language. The statement was, that the name should in some way be connected with "man," "for it is the number of a man," or race of men; "and his number is six hundred three score and six," or 666. As you are aware, the Greeks numbered by means of their letters. Let us, therefore, following the most satisfactory explanation of this ever made, take the Greek letters which give the required number: Λ, 30 + A, 1 + T, 300 + E, 5 + I, 10 + N, 50 + O, 70 + Σ, 200 = 666. We have, thus, the name Lateinos, or Latin man; there being abundant authority for the use of the dipthong ε ι for the Latin long I. Upon the division of the Empire, the word Roman which had formerly prevailed gave way to the words Greek, for the eastern, and Latin, for the western Empire. The term Latin, at first applied only to the language, was adopted by the western Kingdoms. 'It was the Latin world, the Latin Kingdom, the Latin church, the Latin patriarch, the Latin clergy, the Latin councils.' A writer says: 'They Latinize everything: Mass, prayers, hymns; Litanies, canons, decretals, bulls, are conceived in Latin. The Papal councils speak in Latin, women themselves pray in Latin. The scriptures are read in no other language, under the Papacy, than Latin. In short, all things are Latin.' If the characteristics of the beast did not sufficiently place this, the name does.

You will see, then, that the impressions prevailing, and the statements made; that, in some form the papal church is the true church of Christ, that it is the *historic church*, are set aside. The true church —the "woman," which brought forth the truth, with which the truth was really connected, fled into the wilderness; and was hunted and persecuted, and warred against by the powers of the earth, by papal Rome; and the latter—papal Rome—was the *"beast,"* an image verified in the disposition and practices of the papacy—fierce, savage, dreadful, destroying those who opposed it or were at variance with it, seeking to kill the true church of Christ. If you would trace the history of the true church, you must follow the wanderings of the "woman" in the wilderness; those, who, singly or together, worshiped God "in spirit and in truth," clung by faith to the blood of the Lamb, and the word of their testimony, who kept the commandments of God, and loved not their lives unto the death.

There is one pointed omission in connection with the symbol of Ecclesiastical Rome. We are told repeatedly when its temporal authority should cease; the dominion of the first beast being thus given, but not that of the second: this is left *indefinite*. This is not marked by numbers. That influence still lives—now, while the seventh Trumpet is sounding. The great mistake made by second adventists is in naming a time for Christ to appear in bodily form. He said of this: "But of that day and hour knoweth no man, no, not the angels of heaven, but my Father only." Notwithstanding the downfall of the temporal power of the Pope, which may have encouraged some to expect that Christ is now to appear personally; the Scripture gives us to understand that a period—it may be long, shall follow, for the complete and final triumph, by moral weapons, of the true church of the Lord Jesus— now fully out of the wilderness; for even in the city of Rome the pure gospel of Christ is preached to-day, under the very protection of the law of the land. The entrance of Victor Emanuel's army into the city, September 20, 1870, was attended with a load of Bibles.

There were "two horns" to the second beast. One of these I believe to be the church of England, the "Episcopacy." This was at first Romish; all, save in name. Henry VIII. broke with the Pope; but the doctrines of the English church were at first the same as those of the papacy. Persecution was waged by the one as by the other, against heretics. Even now many Episcopalians claim that their church is identical with the Roman Catholic, a "branch" of this; and the tendencies in the one to the practices of the other have been notable, for the last twenty years. At the late General Convention in this country of the Episcopal church, the use of the "crucifix"—that peculiar "mark" of the beast—and of "incense," was quietly but purposely sanctioned. Some, eminent among its clergy, are ready to go farther than this in devotion to Rome. I think I express an accepted fact, when I declare that, however much the mere domination of the Pope is rejected by the mass of Episcopalians, the historic connection with the papacy is a matter of satisfaction as linking their church by a visible historic chain with the far past; and that, in point of doctrine, there is in part a vital identity of the two even now—most prominently as to the "grace of regeneration" in the "sacrament of baptism." Canon Liddon affirms that the doctrines of the "Real presence," "Need of absolution," and of "Reverence for the Saints," are found in the English Prayer book.

IV. *A series of visions*—bright, hopeful, far reaching, is now granted, taking us forward to the consummation of things, to the final victories of God's people, to the reaping time of the Kingdom of Christ.

A new song is sung in heaven, one of the new songs which have rung through the heavenly courts; sung by the elect of God from earth; sung "before the throne, and before the four beasts and the elders." The singers were pure and true followers of Christ; had kept from defilement; were sincere and "without guile" or hypocrisy; were "without fault:" all having been renewed by the blood of the Lamb, were "before the throne of God."

Some five angels now came forth, one after the other.

1. One appeared flying in the midst of heaven "having the everlasting gospel to preach unto them that dwell on the earth, and to every nation, and kindred, and tongue, and people." This chimes in with what we saw at the close of our last lecture. The "kingdoms of the world" were to become "the kingdom of our Lord and of his Christ," this to come to pass in and through the spread of the gospel. We are living at this period of prophetic history, and may favor the great end destined to be reached. Revelation has more to do with this farther along.

2. Another angel followed, saying, "Babylon is

fallen, is fallen." Twice was it declared, as if the angel would say, Babylon is *doubly fallen.* I will not notice now the significance of the use of this name as applied to the beast. A double fall is spoken of, and the truth revealed that as the temporal overthrow had taken place, so the ecclesiastical downfall should come.

3. Another angel announced the spiritual punishment of those who worship "the beast and his image, and receive his mark in forehead or hand." This punishment shall be, the wrath of God poured out without mixture, and shall be eternal; for "the smoke of their torment ascendeth up forever and ever: and they have no rest day nor night who worship the beast and his image, and whosoever receiveth the mark of his name." Here is the faith and the patience of the saints; that they believe the revelation of the end of the evil power, and are patient in view of the seeming long delay of the threatened downfall.

4. From this latter period, it shall be peculiarly blessed to die "in the Lord." This has reference to the millenial time, which is immediately to succeed the second overthrow of Rome. We shall

again notice this. It is declared that as Rome falls, after and through the triumphs of the gospel, a period shall occur when it may be said with peculiar force: "Blessed are the dead which die in the Lord *from henceforth:* yea, saith the spirit, that they may rest from their labors; and their works (or sorrows, through trials) do follow them;" as if these should not be continued upon the earth, but be buried with them; since persecution, and defeat, and wrong, should not go on among the living.

5. Then cometh the end, when Jesus shall appear as on a white cloud, and the angel shall say as from the eternal Father: "Thrust in thy sickle and reap: for the time is come for thee to reap; for the harvest of the earth is ripe. And he that sat on the cloud thrust in his sickle on the earth, and the earth was reaped:" Christ thus gathers his own.

6. "And another angel" "having, also, a sharp sickle," shall come forth; and he shall be directed by the angel of fire, of burning, consuming justice, to reap: "Thrust in thy sharp sickle"—the sickle keen with justice—"and gather the clusters of the vine of the earth; for her grapes are fully ripe. And the angel thrust in his sickle into the earth,

and gathered the vine of the earth, and cast it into the great winepress of the wrath of God. And the winepress was trodden without the city, and blood came out of the winepress, even unto the horses' bridles, by the space of a thousand six hundred furlongs."

Friends, the world is nearing this time. We are hastening toward it. To which do we belong; the harvest of Christ, or the vintage of earth? If the sickle of Christ should now be thrust among men, into our churches, would he gather us to himself, as his own, as "wheat into his garner"? or, should the angel of keen justice cut us off, and cast us into the great winepress of the wrath of God? These are solemn questions—solemn with all the earnestness and importance of the eternal future.

Thank God, ye impenitent, that the angel with the everlasting gospel is still flying in the midst of heaven; and is proclaiming pardon, peace, hope, and safety, to all who do repent, and in their hearts believe on the Lord Jesus Christ. Thank God, that there is still hope for you; and see to it, that your opportunity does not pass misimproved. Oh! now hear and obey the gospel of the Son of God.

I urge you by all the lessons of history; by all the teachings and warnings, the revealings and promises of the word of God; by all the hopes of the gospel, to make your peace with God, your "calling and election sure."

> "Soon will the awful trumpet sound,
>   And call you to his bar;
> His mercy knows the appointed bound,
>   And yields to justice there."

> "Now God invites; how blest the day!
>   How sweet the gospel's charming sound!
> Come, sinners, haste, O haste away,
>   While yet a pard'ning God is found."

VII.

The Seven Last Plagues;

OR,

The Golden Vials and Dreadful Contents.

Revelation, Chapters 15, 16.

IT may surprise you that so many symbols of the Papal power are given in the book of Revelation. But when we consider how important and how large a place it has occupied in the world during the Christian centuries, we shall not wonder at the prominent representation of it in a book picturing these. The fact that this power should be destroyed, the time and general manner of the destruction are given, and have been noticed in several of the preceding lectures. In the Scripture before us now, we are granted a symbolic view of the things which were to have part in its overthrow;

and we shall see that these greatly come under the assertion that the mode of the extinction of its temporal power was the "sword;" while its ecclesiastical domination is to be overcome by the word of God, by moral means. In our next lecture we shall see the reasons for its entire desolation.

The opening of the vision takes us backward, as the last visions we saw formed a compendium of history to the end of time. We shall have no great difficulty in learning the events foreshadowed by the symbols now to come before us.

"Another sign" appeared in heaven, "great and marvelous." Again the number "seven" is given: "seven angels having the seven last plagues" being introduced. According to views already given, the seven would come consecutively, or be so distinct as to be numbered separately; while the added idea of completeness is advanced, as if their work should terminate something; which we find thus far to have been connected with the use of the term. There is this difference between the seven Vials and seven Trumpets and Seals; that the first, unlike the others, are not made the basis of a new seven.

The term "plague" means a wound through a

stripe or blow. The seven Plagues were to have chief bearing upon the beast, as we learn from the victor-song of heaven, and from the place the beast occupies in connection with the plagues. These were to be "last plagues;" as if others had gone before. Finding the first in the revolution of public sentiment in Germany, and the alienation of the German princes from Rome; in the wars of the Dutch Republic and United Netherlands with Spain as the representative of the papacy; and in the dismemberment of England from papal authority—in the sixteenth century; and in the Thirty Years war in Germany—in the seventeenth; as well as in other events and wars which struck at the power of the Pope, and lessened and weakened this: we should look for any plagues that could properly be called "last" plagues, at a time succeeding the others—in, say, the eighteenth and nineteenth centuries; and should expect that these would eventually be final in their effects. Many have recognized that they were to be poured forth in *rapid* succession, even to the seventh.

The *origin* of these Plagues is pointed out as being in the heavenly world, with God. A vision of heaven is spread forth—of "the sea of glass" before the throne of God; seen heretofore, when the door of heaven was first opened to the wondering eyes of John. Now the clear surface of the sea glows "with fire," for it reflects the burning justice and wrath of God, shining from the golden vials, which were soon placed in the hands of the executing angels. There is rejoicing among the saved ones in heaven, especially among those who had gained the victory "over the beast, and over his image, and over his mark," and even "over the number of his name." They stand as representatives of the church in heaven and the church on earth; and, in view of "the judgments of God" "manifest," in the plagues to be poured forth, they sing even prophetically—as is done repeatedly in the progress of the Revelation—the song of victory; the song of deliverance and salvation; the song of Moses, whose foes were overthrown in the sea, and of the Lamb who saves the souls of his people as well as delivers the world of one of its chief enemies, the papal power.

The praise of the victory was given to God, not to man. The song was: "Great and marvelous are thy works, Lord God Almighty: just and true are thy ways, thou King of saints, (or nations,) who shall not fear (or reverence and adore) thee, O Lord, and glorify thy name, for thou only art holy: for all nations shall come and worship before thee: for thy judgments are made manifest." Whatever means should be used, and however undesignedly the agents might act, they should execute the will of God, and should operate in his providence.

The door of the innermost part of the temple was opened. Forth came the seven angels with the Last Plagues in their hands. They were clothed as in "white linen," because they should go forth in righteousness and holiness to their work. They were girded with "golden girdles"—with strength, with "golden" strength—tried and true. A representative of the church, one of the four beasts, gave unto them "seven golden vials (or goblets, or bowls) full of the wrath of God," which became synonymous with the Last Plagues; for it was in pouring forth the wrath that the Plagues fell. What a rebuke this to that hyper, or falsely, charitable spirit which speaks lovingly of Rome, which calls the Pope "that good old man"—falsely charitable because a God, who is love, "pours forth his wrath" upon the one and the other. Note this language, for it goes back of the human to the divine; it gives us an inside view of the papacy, of this as it appears before Him unto whose eyes all things are naked and open.

Nothing should prevent the execution of God's purpose, no intercession check it; for no man was able to enter the temple, till the seven Plagues of the seven angels were fulfilled. The vials containing the wrath were "golden vials," as Lange has so beautifully expressed: The "anger is contained in *golden vials;* it is so scrupulously prepared in heaven, so pondered over, so permeated by the Divine Intelligence, that, as a heroic act of Divine reason, it embodies in itself precisely the opposite to what is described in the heathen pictures of the envy of the gods, and the might of destiny."

"Go!" was now the word to the angels from God within the temple—"Go your ways and pour out the vials of the wrath of God upon the earth."

The order of the Plagues is somewhat like that of the sounding Trumpets; but the particulars are so different that other events are required for the fulfillment of the symbols, a fact which renders the explanation more difficult, and puts to a fresh test the word of God. Be it far from me to force an interpretation of any of these symbols; to try to make a small garment fit a large event, or to cover a small, unimportant thing with a large symbol. My aim is to give you truthful verifications of Divine Pictures. In forming judgment upon some of these, I have been aided by the researches of others who have gone before me in the study of them. I adopt, in part, the conclusions of the lamented Barnes, as to several of the symbols of the Plagues, as of the Seals and Trumpets.

I. " And the first angel went and poured out his vial upon the earth; and there fell a noisome and grievous sore upon the men which had the mark of the beast, and upon them which worshiped his image."

This Plague was to be upon the *earth*, or peculiarly upon the land. It was to come to a special class of men, those who "had the mark of the beast, and who worshiped his image." It was to be like "a noisome, grievous sore"—a polluted, distressing affliction, the outgrowth of an internally diseased condition. As a "boil"—to which reference is had—speaks of a weakened state of the blood; so, this should betray a perverted condition of the mind and moral natures of the persons. It was to come from within themselves, rather than from outside sources.

If the first plagues upon the papal power and its adherents, were associated with the "earthquake" which followed the renewed life of God's witnesses, as recorded in the 11th chapter and 13th verse; and if the commotions and wars which sprang up among the nations, as the human outgrowths of the Reformation, formed those plagues: then we must look for the Seven Last Plagues, as I have said, later than the seventeenth century—in the eighteenth, and, it may be, in the nineteenth.

Let us note, then, again the records of history; for we are again brought to the bearings of general history upon the interpretation of the symbols. Was there any marked event in the eighteenth century, connected with any persons who can be said to have had "the mark of the beast," and to have been "worshipers of his image?" any such people who were afflicted and distressed; yet with a disorder which sprang from within themselves, as from their own blood?

The research is not fruitless; for in all the crowded and vast events of the past few years, the world has not lost sight of an epoch which is still quoted with a shudder by all readers of history. I refer to the French Revolution of 1789. Of all people, the French may be said to have possessed peculiarly the mark of the beast, and to have worshiped his image. They were the first to grant kingly power to the Pope, and have been the last reluctantly, and of necessity to withdraw support from that power; and would gladly, in some of their representatives, in the person of the present Head of the nation, restore the papal domination if they could, and may seek so to do, although the Republican sentiment of France is increasingly against Rome.

What "a noisome, grievous sore" was that event of which we speak as the Revolution of '89! It was from *within*, and it brought to the surface, without curing the nation, an amount of bad passion, of iniquity, of filth, almost incredible. It would not seem to the mind of the philosopher that so much evil could be compressed in human nature, that passion could be so violent, and that injustice should so mark even human hate. The selfishness, the iniquity, the pollution, the bloodshed, can be said to have grown from that professed church whose career has been marked by these. Was France the "eldest son of the church," as the Popes have named it? So, did it nurse its iniquity from its mother's breast; and no wonder, if in the frenzy of its passion, it should—at the time—smite even its mother. Despite all that may be written of the good sought and done in that fearful period, naught shall be able ever to withdraw the eye from the "noisome, grievous sore" which broke out upon the French nation, and attracted and still attracts the horrified gaze of the world; for its horrors have never been equaled in the history of our race.

No more expressive symbol of it could have been given than that of Inspiration, uncovering as this does in a few sentences, by one ghastly picture, not only the evil but the internal source of this; and, as history then and since abundantly shows, all had to do with the downfall of the beast, of papal Rome.

II. "And the second angel poured out his vial upon the sea; and it became as the blood of a dead man; and every living soul died in the sea."

This is a figure of a great calamity falling upon

the *sea;* of naval conflict, which, as it were, reddened the waters of the ocean with the blood of the slain—dead; which utterly devastated it of that power, or those powers connected with the beast: for, we must bear in mind that this Plague, like the first, has to do with the overthrow of Rome. The symbol must find its counterpart, then, in the history of those nations favoring the papacy which were naval powers. The only nations of this character were France, Spain, and Portugal.

Do we find that there was a naval conflict following the French Revolution, and, it may be, growing out of this, in which these nations took part and suffered defeat? In 1793, commenced the naval war between France and England, which lasted twenty years, and involved Spain as well as France. The history of it is thus stated: "There was a series of naval disasters that swept away the fleets of France, and that completely demolished the most formidable naval power that had ever been prepared by any nation under the papal dominion."

From the destruction of the French fleet at Toulon in 1793, to the victory over the Spanish fleet off Cape St. Vincent in 1797; to the great victories of Lord Nelson at the Nile in 1798, at Copenhagen in 1801, and of Trafalgar in 1805; and, onward: in all of which engagements were destroyed some two hundred ships of the line, some three or four hundred frigates, and a large number of small vessels of war and commerce,—from these, is formed a reality of which the symbol of the Second Plague is a faithful reflection. And by as much as it weakened the power of the nations which supported the Pope, by so much did it further the overthrow of his temporal dominion. It has been truly declared of this time, 'that the whole history of the world does not present such a period of naval war, destruction and bloodshed.'

III. "And the third angel poured out his vial upon the rivers and fountains of waters; and they became blood. And I heard the angel of waters" —it may have been, the angel which sounded the third Trumpet—"say, thou art righteous, O Lord, which art, and wast, and shall be, because thou hast judged thus. For they have shed the blood of saints and prophets, and thou hast given them blood to drink; for they are worthy." The word was approved in heaven, for John "heard another out of the altar say, Even so, Lord God Almighty, true and righteous are thy judgments."

The scene changes to "*the rivers and fountains of waters,*" as at the sounding of the Third Trumpet. If that interpretation was correct, then we should look to a similar region for the fulfillment of this symbol; most exactingly, we should turn to the same quarter for its realization. The waters should be, as it were, reddened with blood. The place should be associated with scenes of suffering in the past, an angel recalling that in this very territory had been shed the blood of saints and prophets, or preachers of the gospel; so that for bloodshed to take place here, in such a manner as to inflict injury upon the guilty beast, and to aid in his overthrow, would embody the judgments of God upon a people deserving of such.

In connection with the Third Trumpet we saw that the region of "the rivers and fountains of waters" was that of the Alps and Northern Italy; where, in the valleys of Piedmont, the Waldenses and Albigenses suffered so fearfully from the "beast." If this country was distinguished for any bloody events succeeding the French Revolution—it may be, growing out of this; by any events which had bearing upon that old persecuting power, then the portrait finds its reality; and placing them side by side, we see the features to be the same, the one the picture of the other.

Just such events did follow the French Revolution, in the invasion of Italy under Napoleon. That series of brilliant and bloody victories which marked the opening of his career, which gave him a name, and disclosed to his eyes the possibilities of a great destiny, took place in Northern Italy, where are "the rivers and fountains of waters." In Piedmont, in Lombardy, over the width of Italy, extended the triumphs of the French arms, in a campaign recorded as one of the most memorable in history. The rivers were, indeed, colored with blood, as at the terrible charge at the bridge of Lodi, and at other places along the Po and its tributaries; of the influence of the first of which events on his own mind, Napoleon afterward said: "The 13th Vendemiaire, and the victory of Montenotte did not induce me to believe myself a superior character. It was after the passage of Lodi that the idea shot across my mind that I might become a decisive actor on the political theatre. Then arose, for the first time, the spark of great ambition." He immediately and thereafter acted according to this.

But all the bloodshed of the campaign of '96 was attended with another thing, which completes the verification of the symbol—the revolutionizing of public sentiment in Italy, by means of clubs organized in the cities. The seed was sown which ripened in hostility to the papal power, and has continued to grow; manifesting itself, again and again, as under Mazzini and Garibaldi over twenty years ago, and now in the occupation of Rome by Victor Emanuel, followed by the expressed assent of its citizens.

IV. "And the fourth angel poured out his vial upon the sun; and power was given unto him to scorch men with fire. And men were scorched with great heat, and blasphemed the name of God, which hath power over these plagues: and they repented not to give him glory."

Here the picture of a *sun* is presented. We have seen such to refer heretofore to a great ruling power. A sun was to arise to whom great power should be given, to scorch men with fire—in some form with this; "and men were scorched (or burned) with great heat;" so great should be his blighting influence that men should blaspheme the name of God for permitting such to prevail, yet would continue in impenitence.

I have already spoken a name which appears in the annals of French history, humbly during the Revolution, but raised like a star into the firmament by the Italian campaign—the name of *Napoleon:* who has been called that "demi-god," greater than whose name there is none in all the records of military genius in all the history of the world, and approaching which are only a few that could be counted on the fingers of your two hands. He was but a General in the service of the Republic in his first campaign. But did anything occur which exalted him from a star as into a sun, whose scorching heat fell on "men" generally, irrespective of localities; the fires of whose deeds burned the nations, and caused men, as it were, to blaspheme God?

He was so elevated. He was placed at the head of the French nation as First Consul; but he subsequently secured Imperial dignity, and became the Emperor of the French. As such he led armies, officered by Marshals, who—both officers and men—are, again and again, spoken of as burning with impatience for battle; and whose blazing artillery and musketry, and clashing steel, scorched men as with fire, burned and consumed them.

But, as if to render the likeness most striking; as if to make the reality and the symbol as *"twin-suns,"* double-suns, in Revelation and history, we read that on that morning in Austria, when the French forces were confronted by the combined armies of Austria and Russia, led by the Emperors of these in person; as the blow was about to be struck which prostrated Europe before the French power, "the sun rose in unclouded brilliancy." Not a strange thing, indeed; but it attracted the eye of Napoleon, so that he subsequently identified it with himself and his career, apostrophizing the "*Sun* of Austerlitz" as "illuminating the most splendid periods of his life."

This is a most remarkable verification of the Scripture symbol. The victory gained at Austerlitz bore upon the condition of Italy, to determine divisions formed there being the immediate cause of the war; a victory, followed by a career which filled the world with wonder and with suffering; and which, from first to last, as extended from the Mediterranean to the Baltic, from the heats of Egypt and Palestine to the snows of Russia, from the Atlantic inward, was as a burning sun, blasting men with the fires of war.

That Napoleon's successes struck at the beast, is manifest—among other things—from the fact that one of his campaigns resulted in the compulsory renouncement by the Emperor of Austria of the title of "Emperor of the Holy Roman Empire and of Germany."

But, notwithstanding all this, French infidelity spread almost the world over, even sweeping up and over our own shores like a tidal wave. "Men repented not to give God glory" in the midst of their sufferings, or when the sun went down over Waterloo, and behind the rocky heights of St. Helena.

V. "And the fifth angel poured out his vial upon the seat of the beast; and his kingdom was full of darkness; and they gnawed their tongues with pain, and blasphemed the God of heaven because of their pains and their sores, and repented not of their deeds."

A definite locality is anew mentioned, "*the seat of the beast*," which we have seen to be the city of Rome; "and his kingdom." This was "full of darkness," the symbol of distress; but the destruction of the power was not pictured. What should occur would be momentary. "Pains and sores" should be suffered; "pains" as from an outside hand, should be inflicted; but the trouble should, also, be internal, as in connection with the first Plague.

We must again turn our eyes toward Rome, "the seat of the beast." Looking thither at a time subsequent to the breaking out of the French Revolution, and after the first Italian campaign, but before the "sun of Austerlitz" arose; we find a condition of things, in some respects remarkable. If almost any nation but the French had brought it about, it would not have been so strange; but that Catholic France should turn, at any time, against the temporal power of the Pope, was singular. I think that the order of time is reversed in this one instance because of a design to reach a climax in the representations of the downfall of the Pope.

The effort at first made was to revolutionize the Papal States. Pius VI. was an old man, and not expected to live. Joseph Bonaparte, French Ambassador at Rome, was given instructions to allow, at the Pope's death, no successor to be elected to the chair of St. Peter; and the President of the Directory wrote to Napoleon: "In regard to Rome, the Directory cordially approve of the instructions you have given to your brother, to prevent a successor being appointed to Pius VI. *We must lay hold of the present favorable circumstances to deliver Europe of the pretended papal supremacy.*" Occasion offered, revolution was organized, and the French were invited to enter Rome. Doing so, they ordered the Pope to depart; and used personal violence with him. He was dragged from the very altar of his palace; the rings, torn from his fingers; and he was finally compelled to journey to France, traversing "often during the night the Apennines and the Alps, in a rigorous season," and surviving his arrival at Valence only ten days.

Great was the spoliation which followed the occupation of Rome by the French. Surely, "pains" from without and "sores" from within became the portion of the people; and great was the "darkness" which extended over the kingdom of the beast, yet the people of this "repented not of their deeds." Here, then, were realities which accord with the symbol before us; and, although, in this one case the order of time, for a good reason, was reversed, the events were distinct; and, as such, have a place in history as in Revelation.

If it be insisted that the symbol should meet a fulfillment at a latter date than the Austerlitz campaign; then do we behold the realization of it, in the renewed dethronement of the Pope by Napoleon, in the year 1809; when the Roman States were incorporated with the French Empire. In either case it was only "darkness" that was experienced by the "kingdom," a temporary obscuring of the papal power; which was, after a few years, again restored.

VI. "And the sixth angel poured out his vial upon the *great river Euphrates;* and the water thereof was dried up, that the way of the kings of the east might be prepared. And I saw three unclean spirits like frogs come out of the mouth of the dragon, and out of the mouth of the beast, and out of the mouth of the false prophet. For they are the spirits of devils, working miracles, which go forth to the kings of the earth and of the whole world, to gather them to the battle of that great day of God Almighty. Behold, I come as a thief. Blessed is he that watcheth, and keepeth his garments, lest he walk naked, and they see his shame. And he gathered them together into a place called in the Hebrew tongue Armageddon."

There are several features to this symbol, and the scenes of the things pictured are separated. The power which sprang from the river Euphrates is plainly introduced, and the drying up of the waters of the river presents a gradual disappearance of that power; and thus "the way of the kings of the east is prepared." These kings are not brought forward specially; only, events progress which prepare their way—for what purpose, is not stated. As applied to any power the symbol would speak of the decline of this, or the extinction of its people. This forms one feature of the diverse picture. Another, is the appearance of "three unclean spirits like frogs," which come "out of the mouth of the dragon, and out of the mouth of the beast, and out of the mouth of the false prophet." It is not said that one came out of the mouth of each, but the three were associated with all; and they were "unclean." They were evil forces, "for they are the spirits of devils;" they work what would be called miracles, and "they go forth unto the kings of the earth and of the whole world," "to gather them to the battle of the great day of God Almighty," which latter was to take place at a future time, account of which we find in the 19th chapter of the book. This time should be one when watchfulness and carefulness would be specially called for,— watchfulness against subtle, deceiving evil; carefulness, as to personal godliness. The one other lineament of the picture is the place, where should be gathered the forces of the world, led by the unclean spirits, which was "called in the Hebrew tongue Armageddon;" the name being used, doubtless, figuratively, as we have thus found the names Sodom and Egypt employed in previous revelations.

The power referred to will be readily recognized as that which came at first from the Euphrates, and which we viewed in connection with the sounding of the sixth Trumpet—that of the Turks. We should naturally have expected that its future destiny would be set forth. Here we learn this. Bear in mind the order of *time*, when we should look for the fulfillment of the picture. It would not antedate the symbols already explained; if in part synchronous, we should naturally count upon its going beyond the others. Do we find that the Turkish power has been in any special manner weakened, and that it has continued to decrease, within, say, the last fifty or one hundred years? From history we learn that in the year 1683 the Turks, 300,000 strong, invaded Austria. John Sobieski of Poland, the champion of Christendom, hastened with only 18,000 men to the relief of Vienna; and when united with the allies he had only 70,000 men: yet with these he assailed the vast Turkish horde, and achieved a victory which "broke the Mussulman power so effectually, that for the first time for three hundred years the crescent of Mohammed permanently receded, and from that period historians date the decline of the Ottoman Empire." Dating subsequent to the events of the symbols of previous Plagues, then we must reckon from the year 1815, when Waterloo was fought. Then you should find a great cause of the decline

of the Turkish power to have been "internal revolt
and insurrection," which took place in the year
1820. Following this was the Greek insurrection
which resulted in the independence of Greece;
England, France and Russia, aiding in securing this
in the year 1827. Internal decay has gone forward;
the country is being drained to people Constantinople, where the new comers find the pit of corruption and death. The way of the kings of the east is
being prepared, and the drying up of the Turkish
rule, as of the Euphrates, is the preparation; which
decline is taking place, despite the combined aid of
England and France rendered in the Crimean war
to uphold Turkey as against Russia, and notwithstanding the assistance given to the Ottoman Empire by the European powers both in Syria and
Egypt. It may have gained a few African tribes
during the last thirty years; and in some places,
the census—by doubtful comparisons, however—
may show an increase of Mussulman population;
but its political and military strength are on the
wane, and only the intervention of the great nations
of Europe has preserved to it vast portions of its
territory, and saved it from greater humiliation.

The decrease of its political might means the drying up of its religious sway; for, with it, the two are inseparably connected. A thing may be said to be dried up, when a diversion renders it void of force. May we not look for the preparation of the kings of the east, also, in the application of steam to commerce; whereby the way to the west is more fully opened to the eastern nations? The kings of the east, "*beyond* the Euphrates"—for this is the intent of the scripture—turn their eyes eastward to America; and over the highway of the Pacific are passing thousands of their people; while the agencies of the gospel are making their way to the eastern lands without reference to the old boundaries, with scarcely a thought of the Euphrates.

The three devilish spirits which were seen to proceed out of the "mouth of the dragon, out of the mouth of the beast, and out of the mouth of the false prophet," were—I believe—Slavery, Mormonism, and Spiritism. If the "dragon" stands for pagan Rome, then I point you to the fact that spiritism traces its history back among the mystic rites and oracles of Paganism. That slavery is in harmony with the "beast," is seen in the fact that the Pope approved this by his recognition of the Southern Confederacy; and that the "false prophet" may be represented as sending forth a kindred spirit, is seen in the history of Mormonism in this country. Whether these things are "unclean," like frogs, I leave for you to judge; that all could be said to come from each, and each from all, their records attest. But the question of time, which we must persistently keep before us, settles it. We look for their appearance after the year 1820, when we may certainly date the decline of the Turkish power; and surprising is the response which the last fifty years gives to the symbol. Slavery had existed among us, but it was not earnestly and generally recognized in its true character until about the year 1831; when that agitation of the subject began, which, rising from the people, extended into the church and state, leading to the organization of society after society—social and churchly, and finally of political party; the culmination being the civil war, amid which the evil thing was crushed beneath the trampling of a million feet, and the roll of artillery which belched forth the doom of the institution as such. Near the time that the spirit of slavery was evoked, Mormonism took its rise, in the pretensions of Joe Smith. If spiritism had prevailed before, it appeared anew, in the year 1848—and with marvelous deceptive power, through its so-called spiritistic phenomena—and swept onward, going forth to assemble the world, if possible, against Christianity. These things have gathered the people, and have been made up of a medley of these.

Surely, all this has been a time when men needed to watch and "keep their garments," a time of delusion; Slavery, Mormonism, and Spiritism, trying the very church of Christ, testing the watchfulness and fidelity of God's true people.

But the *place* where these forces should be gathered, and where they should gather the people, is deserving of attention. "He (or they) gathered them together into a place called in the Hebrew tongue Armageddon;" having reference to Megiddo, or the plain of Esdrælon. This is the only time the name is used in the New Testament. Its use was figurative. It should be an appropriate representation of a place, at the time foreshadowed. Armageddon was the Old Testament battle field; the great battle-ground of God's people with their enemies. It was a natural gathering place, a highway from the east to the west, the west to the east. It was a world's battle-field; it has been a scene of strife in all the ages. A writer declares that 'warriors out of every nation which is under heaven have pitched their tents in the plain of Esdrælon, and have beheld the various banners of their nations wet with the dews of Tabor and Hermon.' Here fought Barak and Sisera, Gideon and the Midianites, Josiah and the Egyptians; here was encamped the army of Nebuchadnezzar, here Vespasian battled with the Jews; here Crusaders and Saracens butchered each other, and here an army of Turks was defeated by the French under Napoleon and Kleber. The scene is a most striking figure of a place where should be a gathering of the nations, and where a great moral warfare should take place; for it is such that we are to understand to be meant, from the leaders in the combined forces of evil. The strife of principles might even merge into a conflict of arms. Where shall we look for such a place, at the time of the fulfilled symbol—in the nineteenth century; where, if not *to America?* I think, without a doubt, that this is intended; and we have only to turn to the history of our country for the last fifty years, to see the vivid realization of the Divine Picture. No other place than Armageddon were so graphic a likeness of this land; no other land so fully answers the spiritual significance of that Hebrew name and place as this. It is in this light—as a battle-ground of principles—that America shall come to be more and more regarded.

VII. "And the seventh angel poured out his vial into the air; and there came a great voice out of the temple of heaven, from the throne, saying, It is done," the work of destruction is now to be completed. The voice, evidently of God's providence, is followed by "voices and thunders, and lightnings; and there was a great earthquake, such as was not since men were upon the earth, so mighty an earthquake, and so great." Commotions and convulsions are here portrayed, the greatness of which is to be measured by the principles involved as truly as by the outward phenomena. To say that such have occurred, is only to repeat the history of the past fifteen years. There have been "voices," the booming "thunders" and flashing "lightnings" of war; of wars unsurpassed in their magnitude; an overturning, as by an "earthquake," of ruling powers and of long established institutions. Witness, the wars of Europe, and the changes in the predominant powers, nations long conceded to be invincible in military prowess, losing their prestige in brief campaigns, before such a concentration of troops as never before was known in the history of the world. Witness, the overthrow of slavery in our own land, which fifteen years ago seemed to be a thing of the far future, a thing scarcely to be realized; so did the nation honestly feel and declare: but violently has it been cast down. To say that so mighty an earthquake, and so great, in its bearings and in itself, has not taken place since men were upon the earth, is no exaggeration of language; as a figure of speech, it finds its verity in the events of our own day.

"The great city was divided into *three parts.*" We are to understand by this, as when a "tenth part of the city" fell; that the powers, which—united with the papacy—sustained this, were three; which we find literally to have been the case. There was Rome, Austria and France. By the intervention and aid of the two latter, Garibaldi was dispossessed of Rome in 1849, and the Pope restored to his dominions. By their help Rome was sustained thereafter. But "the cities of the nations fell"—the cities of these two nations fell, which was most markedly substantiated in the wars of 1866 and 1870-'71; when city after city gave way, the conflicts greatly centering at these. In the defeat at Sadowa, the cities of Austria were virtually prostrated. Within fourteen days after the French government called out the army of reserves against Prussia, fourteen cities were proclaimed in a state of siege. From Strasburg on the east, to Sedan, to Metz, to Paris on the farther west, did the decisive operations take place at the cities of France. That these were intended is most manifest; for with their fall "great Babylon came in remembrance before God": he, as it were, remembered that the time had come, of which he had spoken by the mouth of his servants the prophets, and which Christ had foretold his servant John, and through him his people and the world. "Unto her" was given "the cup of the fierceness of his wrath," which she drank, as her temporal power ceased. "Every island fled away, and the mountains were not found"—fled away from her, were not found to help her; so, the small powers and the great, the "islands" and the "mountains" or great kingdoms, forsook her.

The manner in which all the overthrows were effected, the cities of the nations fell, and Babylon came to be forsaken and to go down, is given. "And there fell upon men a *great hail out of heaven*, every stone about the weight of a talent: and men blasphemed God because of the plagues of the hail; for the plague thereof was exceeding great." It was thus that the plague was "poured into the *air*." To have been under the fierce *bombardments* of the late war in our own land, and to know that such had so large a place in the Franco-Prussian war; to rememember that thus Strasburg, and finally Paris were reduced, opens our eyes to see the plague of the air, which would lead men to blaspheme God. Even the battle of Sedan is described by an eye witness, as "essentially an affair of artillery." The air crowded with great missiles—hissing, screaming, bursting; falling among men—terrifying, mangling, killing; stones full "a talent's weight"—or fifty-six pounds, more than averaging this: most certainly meets the requirements of the symbol, and shows us that all the seven plagues have been poured forth, accomplishing their designed and prophesied effect, of destroying the "beast," even corroborating the prophetic time of this.

As favoring the view that Providence designed that now should end the temporal power of the Pope, is a side scene. Mexico, from the time of Cortes, for three hundred years and more, had been a Catholic country; this, alone. Notwithstanding the independence gained from Spain fifty years ago, the papal religion was maintained. The Revolution embraced as one of its principles the exclusive prevalence of this. But in the civil war, subsequent to our war with Mexico, and which followed the interference of the Authorities of that country with the monasteries in the city of Mexico, the power of the church was weakened. Taking advantage of the rebellion in the United States, Maximilian was sent to Mexico; not so much by Napoleon as by the Pope. The triumph of this movement against the Republican rulers, meant the victory of the papal church, and the existence of a nation in America which should be allied to Rome, and which should sustain this. But the close of our war left our army ready to enforce the Monroe doctrine; and 60,000 men under Sherman and Sheridan, being sent to the Rio Grande, Napoleon was requested to withdraw his troops from American soil, which he very politely did. Maximilian relying upon the church party, reluctantly remained; was captured by the Republican forces, and executed. Upon the spot where he fell, a rude mound of stones now stands, bearing the marks of crosses, and pointing to the virtual grave of papacy in Mexico; which country is now open to evangelization, and where the forces of Christ and Anti-Christ are to contend, with no uncertainty as to the result. The year which really dates the downfall of Maximilian and the church party, is the year 1866, when the French troops were re-called from the country; as if God would say to the papacy: "Thus far shalt thou come, but no farther."

You will be impressed with the fact that so many of the symbols of the book before us have been fulfilled—to the seventh Seal, opening into the sounding Trumpets; to the seventh Trumpet, sounding now, as the seven Plagues have been poured forth.

These last, I believe, have all been inflicted; and we shall soon be called to look upon events connected really with the continued sounding of the seventh Trumpet. We are permitted to think, then, of by far the larger portion of the book of Revelation as we do of the Old Testament prophecies; with the difference, that the interest in the fulfillment of the Divine Pictures of the Christian Centuries is fresher because the verification is more recent, and, thus, seemingly, more forcible.

You will have marked that God has to do with human history; that events for which men blaspheme him, though for which they should repent and give glory to him, are of his permissive and direct providence. The world is linked to his throne, and he "doeth his will in the armies of heaven and among the inhabitants of the earth." He has his ways to overturn the throne of iniquity; and in the events of the past few years, as of all the ages, we are to see his hand. Most remarkable was the oft repeated recognition of this by the great ruler of that nation which has had so much to do with the fulfillment of God's will at the present day—by the now Emperor William, who, in dispatch after dispatch, as victory followed victory to his arms, owned the providence and goodness of God, and gave glory to him.

"Sentence against an evil work" may long be delayed, but in God's time, foreknown and predetermined, he shall overcome and destroy this. The subject has a lesson to us personally; to you as sinners before God. The forces of destruction are already appointed; the sentence has been pronounced: only, the day of execution awaits. Repent, then, and seek pardoning mercy through the blood of the Lamb; lest his justice fall upon you, and there be "none to deliver."

VIII.
The Babylon Woman; or, Fallen Harlot.

Revelation, Chapters 17, 18.

WE have thus far in our Lectures placed ourselves in thought beside the aged apostle in his exile, have noted the words and appearance of the Divine Artist, and have read his appointed Letters to the churches. As the rolls of the Unsealèd Book have been spread forth, we have opened the scroll of human history and found that the characters on each were akin. We have listened to the Trumpets sounding through the corridors of Time, the notes blending—like the different parts of music—with the sounds of earthly events; the harsh, woeful forebodings being relieved by the voice of "mighty angel" speaking in blessing to the world, the strain echoing past us, and floating onward until it mingles with the music of thanksgiving over "the kingdoms of this world, become the kingdom of our Lord and of his Christ."

Under the sunlight of Christ's countenance, we saw the Glorious Woman who was bathed with his beams and reflected these from crown of stars and shining footstool, and brought to its birth the New Testament of our Lord Jesus Christ. The light of Revelation disclosed to us the early fearful conflict between truth and error; and the dreadful Dragon in his repeated and malignant workings; and the Wild-Beast, in its fierce goings forth against God's true people, doubling its development and becoming as two beasts, one of which was to outlive the other: while, as if to relieve the last, dark pictures, the rays of divine light dart forward into the far future and clothe the summits of the distant hills, though the valleys between are to our eyes filled with mist; we knowing that this shall be dissipated, and assured that the sun is to shine upon them in glory.

Then, after Seal and Trumpet, after Glorious Woman, Fierce Strife, Warring Beasts, and glad words of prophecy of the final issue of events, civil or ecclesiastical, the eye is attracted to the Golden

Vials whose dreadful contents are poured forth by angel hands, inflicting God's righteous anger upon the "beast."

If the "Seven Last Plagues" were to destroy and have destroyed the temporal power of Rome, there yet remains its vast ecclesiastical organization, working as we full well know in this country most zealously and in the old world as earnestly. Has Revelation nothing to say of this? no pictures to foreshadow this?

We should naturally expect, according to the rules of interpretation followed, that, if the intention was to reproduce in the chapters now before us anything already given; while there would be features sufficiently marked to identify the present image with others previously sketched, there would be also, a carrying forward of the thing symbolized into a still future time. Such do we find; and that a change occurs which presents the old Wild-Beast most prominently in the form of a *woman*—identified, in history with the beast, but now raised above this, as claiming chief notice.

If this new representation is a picture of another era in the history of the papacy, following the downfall of its temporal might, something special should characterize it; as was true of the rise of the first beast and of the second, the one coming forth at the beginning of the seventh century, the other at the council of Trent in the sixteenth. Is there any fresh development of it, calling special attention to itself; so that men should be led to designate it even as a "New Departure?" Most marvelously do we learn this to be so; that the words which were the signal of the overthrow of its temporal power, mark, also, a new period in the papacy, and present this in a light justifying another resemblance of which prophetic intimations had been already given. The Vatican Decrees of 1870 indicate a new era in Rome, and give us to see the similarity of the papacy as this now exists with the symbol of the 17th chapter—to see it more fully than ever could have been done before; moreover, as maturing for its final doom. Say what Romanists will about the past claim to the Infallibility of the Pope, facts prove that this was disputed even in their church, and was not a part of its creed. If the doctrine has long grown in the purpose of the hierarchy, it has only now ripened and appeared fully asserted;

and points the third and last phase of the papacy : for "in reaching the summit of its power, the papacy has hastened its downfall."

I. The chief picture now sketched is that of "*a Woman.*" "The woman is that great city which reigneth over the kings of the earth." She is a "mystery," or, has a mystical name, which is "Babylon, the great;" for just what Babylon was in the world in its time, so should this woman be in her day. The word "Mystery" was at one time inscribed on the Pope's tiara. You will see that the woman now depicted is not the Glorious Woman viewed in connection with the twelfth chapter. Everything about her is different, and she is identified with the Beasts that warred against that other woman. The contrast is as great as that of Babylon and Jerusalem, a good and a bad woman. She is not called *the* woman, for this article is omitted; she is named "a woman."

Let us view the woman now portrayed. There was certainly something very imposing about her outwardly. She was so robed and appeared to be so great as to excite the great and wondering admiration of the Christian seer; just as the reality set forth has addressed itself to the eyes of men, in that long history and far reaching influence and power which this has had among the nations. Like some old cathedral, appealing to our minds, by its very age and its ancient and long accumulated adornments, does the papacy impress men with reverence; these overlooking, in the former instance, that the temple may be pagan, and in the latter, that a thing is not necessarily true because old, and that an organization may long endure through the strength of sin and satan, as truly as through the power of holiness and God: albeit, it must, in the former case, finally give way. Though the papacy were as old as Babylon; it is, also, portrayed by Divine hand as being likewise corrupt.

A name is applied to the woman which may seem harsh, severe, dreadful; but it is used again and again, and we know that for the employment of it there must be ample justification: else, the Lord would not have put it into the mouth of a man, much less into the mouth of an angel. She is called "a great whore," the "mother of harlots and abominations of the earth." Harlotry is an epithet given in scripture to cities and peoples that are unfaithful, idolatrous, and corrupt. This woman is exhibited not only as debased herself, but as tainting others; not simply sensually, but intellectually, socially, and morally. She aspired to association with kings, with nations; and with her "the kings of the earth have committed fornication, and the inhabitants of the earth have been made drunk with the wine of her fornication." She sat "upon many waters," as if these were at her feet, as the waves of the ocean rolling in upon the shore, and over which she had dominion; these being afterward explained as, "peoples, and multitudes, and nations, and tongues."

Of the appropriateness of the latter simile to the papal church, there can be no doubt. The time has been when all the peoples and multitudes and nations and tongues, were under her, as subjects under a mistress—all but the few unknown, at times, by man, whose names were written in the Lamb's book of life. Look we over the world to-day, and we behold that in almost every nation and among "the peoples, and multitudes, and tongues," she asserts her power; some lands being still almost wholly under her sway. That she has sought fellowship with kings is one of the most pointed of historic facts. Even now when her temporal power has passed away, the desire and claim to this are cherished; and may be again pressed even at the point of the bayonet, and proclaimed by the loud-mouthed cannon. There is no question but that to gain a kind of dominion from which Jesus turned, and the desire for which he repressed in his disciples, the Pope and his minions would consent to the slaughter of human life, just, as it now appears, they have done in the past.

But has her association with the kings of the earth, with the nations and the inhabitants personally, been debasing? I point you to all history for reply. That the Roman Catholic nations have been ignorant, debased socially, corrupt morally; that papal Rome has been a source of evil, and of final decay, is true. The more intimate the connection, the more dreadful the result. It has blighted the fairest lands on earth. Wherever her power has extended, all forms of evil have prevailed; and only as nations have thrown off her domination and influence, have they risen intellectually, socially and morally. Mr. Macaulay, who was a better historian and essayist than prophet, thus wrote of this effect:

'During the last three centuries, to stunt the growth of the human mind has been her chief object. Throughout Christendom, whatever advance has been made in knowledge, in freedom, in wealth, and in the arts of life, has been made in spite of her— and has everywhere been in inverse proportion to her power. The loveliest and most fertile provinces of Europe have, under her rule, been sunk in poverty, in political servitude, and in intellectual torpor; while Protestant countries, once proverbial for sterility and barbarism, have been turned by skill and industry into gardens, and can boast of a long list of heroes and statesmen, philosophers and poets. Whoever, knowing what Italy and Scotland naturally are, and what, four hundred years ago, they actually were, shall now compare the country around Rome with the country around Edinburgh, will be able to form some judgment as to the tendency of papal domination. The descent of Spain, once the first among monarchies to the lowest depths of degradation—the elevation of Holland, in spite of many natural disadvantages, to a position such as no commonwealth so small has ever reached, teach the same lesson. Whoever passes in Germany from a Roman Catholic to a Protestant principality, in Switzerland from a Roman Catholic to a Protestant canton, in Ireland from a Roman Catholic to a Protestant county, finds that he has passed from a lower to a higher grade of civilization. On the other side of the Atlantic the same law prevails. The Protestants of the United States have left far behind them the Roman Catholics of Mexico, Peru, and Brazil. The Roman Catholics of Lower Canada remain inert, while the whole continent round them is in a ferment with Protestant activity and enterprise. The French have doubtless shown an energy, and an intelligence which, even when misdirected, have justly entitled them to be called a great people. But this apparent exception, when examined, will be found to confirm the rule; for in no country that is called Roman Catholic, has the Roman Catholic church, during several generations, possessed so little authority as in France.'

The region pronounced to be the most corrupt in all the world, is that of Rome and the former papal dominions. The nearer the people to that "holy father," the Pope, the more unholy they are or become; and the countries which come next in order of importance as papal nations, approximate nearest in such notoriety. Catholics would fain lay the responsibility of the present condition of Rome morally upon other shoulders; and speak of the open iniquities of the place. But, be it remembered, that Protestants have but just entered Rome; that a Protestant sanctuary was not until recently permitted within the walls of the city; that Rome and Italy are what they are because of their long subjection to the "holy see;" and that the Rome of to-day meets its equal in the Rome of the sixteenth century, when it was proverbially the wickedest place on the face of the earth. Romanists will extol the virtue of the city, because of its complete submission to the papacy in other days; but it was even then the Rome of the stiletto, and a city of secret sin; the city of the Inquisition, albeit, a very large proportion of its inhabitants were ecclesiastics.

John was "carried away in the spirit into the *wilderness;*" he was led to see the Babylon Woman at a time when she could be said to be in a wilderness. This has been judged to represent the Roman Campagna, which surrounds the city with drear, desolate wastes. Whatever the literal intent of the word, if such there be to this, how different this wilderness from the one into which the Glorious Woman, of the 12th chapter, fled. That opened, as in valleys, to receive the hunted woman; but this wilderness betrays desolate surroundings, and evidently symbolized a time when the second woman pictured should be wasted. What time, or what portion of her history could be better called a wilderness than the present, as she is deserted by all the nations who have heretofore favored her?

Taken into the wilderness, John saw her sitting "upon a *scarlet colored beast.*" It is declared to be "remarkable that nothing would better represent the favorite color at Rome than this, or the actual appearance of the Pope, the Cardinals, and the Priests in their robes, on some great festival occasion." "This is the color of the dress of the Cardinals, their hats and cloaks and stockings being always of this color. It is the color of the carriages of the Cardinals, the entire body of the carriage being scarlet, and the trappings of the horses, the same. On occasion of public festivals and processions, scarlet is suspended from the windows of the houses along which the processions pass. The inner color of the cloak of the Pope is scarlet; his carriage is scarlet: the carpet on which he treads is scarlet." This color attracts the attention of all travelers who visit Rome and are present at festal times; and affords a most vivid verification of the symbol.

The woman was seen to be "*full of the names of blasphemy,*" the term "full" being remarkable in its emphasis, as if *all* the names of blasphemy had been assumed. The Jews said that Christ blasphemed because he called himself the "Son of God," thus making himself "equal with God." But it was not blasphemy in him; for he "thought it not robbery to be equal with God," since he was "the brightness of the Father's glory and the express image of his person;" of whom it was said: "Thy throne, O God, is forever and ever." But what shall be said of sinful man being thus extolled? Yet so do we find the Pope to have been exalted by Roman Catholic writers. He has been named: 'Our Lord God the Pope. Another God upon earth, King of kings and Lord of lords. The same is the dominion of God and the Pope. To believe that our Lord God the Pope might not decree as he decreed, is heresy. The power of the Pope is greater than all created power, and extends itself to things celestial, terrestrial, and infernal. The Pope doeth whatsoever he listeth, even things unlawful, and is more than God.' To say that these things are not sanctioned by the Pope or the papal church, is to contradict the decree of Infallibility lately approved.

"The seven heads and ten horns" were explained in our lecture on the Beasts. They are again noticed in the interpretation by the angel, and would be recognized as the same as those before witnessed.

The woman was gorgeously attired, "arrayed in purple and scarlet color, and decked with gold and precious stones, and pearls," a comparison most natural to a church which thus clothes its officials, and thus decks its altars; for, go to whatever country you will, where the papacy prevails, or go to whatever neighborhoods you may, however mean or filthy, where is a Catholic church; entering this, you will find the effort at display of riches manifest. I have noted this in our land, on the Atlantic and Pacific coasts, in the Canadas, in Cuba, on the Isthmus; and what is to be seen on this continent will scarcely compare with the magnificence of the priestly robes and cathedral altars of the old world. The desire for rich vestments and wealthy surroundings forms one of the chief ambitions of the papacy.

"The cup in her hand" appears in a medal struck by the papacy itself. It was a sign of sacramental sanctity; but its contents, in this instance, reveals it as a cup of hypocrisy: for, though golden in appearance, and clean on the outside, it was "full of abominations and filthiness of her fornications."

. The "Mystery"—connected with the name given to her—is that "mystery of iniquity" of which Paul spoke; and was, also, called by the angel Christ, in chapter 10, "the mystery of God," because he knew it, and had foretold it to his servants the prophets. It was well named "Babylon," as the seat of Empire; appearing in its time, at the head of the world—proud, arrogant, oppressive, marked by a subjugation of all to its control, and by its desolating power. What Babylon and pagan Rome were to the world, so was papal Rome to this.

But she was a "*drunken* woman," " drunken with the blood of the saints, and with the blood of the martyrs of Jesus." 'The phraseology is derived from the barbarous custom (still extant among many pagan nations) of drinking the blood of enemies slain in the way of revenge. The effect of drinking blood is said to be to exasperate, and to intoxicate with passion and with a desire of revenge.' We need not look again to the pages of history to see that this condition has been brought about by the excess of blood which papal Rome has, as it were, drank; so that reason has been destroyed, conscience perverted, heart corrupted, and sensual passion come to predominate.

This is the picture of the Woman we are called to view. I think that this whole symbol, which in this part, is completed in the 6th verse of the 17th chapter, casts upon the canvas the features of the papal church *as we see it in our day;* a general portrait, indeed, of that church, but of this as and after the Plagues are poured forth. What follows—the explanation by the angel, reveals this more fully; as well as presents an epitome of her history from the first to the last of her temporal dominion; and, finally, the prophetic vision of her spiritual downfall. The kings of the earth are seen to "have committed fornication with her, and the inhabitants of the earth have been made drunk with the wine of her fornication;" and the woman was "*full* of names of blasphemy:" no more could be added; the last, affixed in our day—the claim of the divine attribute of Infallibility, filling the infamous list. The cup in her hand was "*full* of abominations and filthiness of her fornications;" and she was now "*drunken* with the blood of saints, and with the blood of the martyrs of Jesus," having reached the extreme of her career.

II. The second division of the entire subject, is found in the *explanation given by the angel to the wondering apostle*. More light is thrown upon the canvas, and the features which link the present to other symbols appear; and further evidence is afforded that we are looking at the papal church after the Seven Plagues have been poured forth: although, indeed, it is one of the angels of the Plagues which points to the bloody Woman that is to be destroyed as such. She is identified with the "beast," though this ceases to be most prominent.

This oneness we learn, when, in a word, its history is given. "The beast was, and is not; and shall ascend out of the bottomless pit and go into perdition; and they that dwell on the earth shall wonder, whose names were not written in the book of life from the foundation of the world, when they behold the beast that *was, and is not,* and YET IS." The beast was to exist; then perish, as we have seen it now to have done; and, though again coming forth, it is to "go into perdition," which latter event is revealed in vision in the 19th chapter and 20th verse, where reference is had, doubtless, to the future destruction of the spiritual power of the beast. Hence, the "beast was," as a temporal power; "is not," as such, now; "yet is" a living force in the world, in the form of the Woman, the papal *church.*

We need not notice minutely again the description of the Beast and Woman. It is given once more in Revelation that the relation of the two might be plain; indeed, this is positively declared, for the woman is said to be "that great city which reigneth over the kings of the earth." The peculiarities here stated accord with the other representations. There are "seven kings," or dynasties. At the time the apocalypse was given, five had fallen; kings, consuls, dictators, decemvirs, and military tribunes. The one then existing was the imperial, or sixth; that which arose after this, and "continued a short space," comparatively, was the dukedom under the exarchate of Ravenna; and the eighth which was of the seven, was the papal dominion, and sprang up amid the others and supplanted these. The kingdoms which received power "one hour," or the "same hour," with the beast, were the kingdoms which followed the old Empire. "These with one mind gave their power and strength unto the beast;" and with her, "made war with the Lamb:" and the Lamb should overcome them. A strange feature of the symbol here, is that the ten horns should "hate the whore," and make her "desolate and naked," and "eat her flesh, and burn her with fire;" as we see to have been greatly fulfilled: the very nations which supported Rome turning against her, desolating and consuming her; absorbing her into themselves, as Italy, aided by Germany, has finally completely accomplished. God permitted them "to agree and give their kingdoms unto the beast, until the words of God should be fulfilled;" which they have done, protecting her substantially through the 1260 years, and withdrawing their help, per desire and necessity, in these days of realized prophecy. In confirmation of this, are recent words of Archbishop McCluskey who declares: "Kings, princes, potentates, are united in their powerful opposition against the Pontiff in the see of Peter."

You have thus the symbol of the Woman—of the papal church as we now see this; together with an explanation which links her with the "beasts" of the past, and which touches upon marked phases of her history.

III. Next view the *fall of this Babylon Woman*.

"After these things, I saw another angel come down from heaven, having great power; and the earth was lightened with his glory. And he cried mightily with a strong voice, saying Babylon, the great *is fallen, is fallen*, and is become the habitation of devils, and the hold of every foul spirit, and a cage of every unclean and hateful bird." The picture is taken from the dreadfully desolate condition of the city of Babylon in its overthrow. As this was a symbol of papal Rome in other things, so was it to be such in its destruction. It has been looked upon as haunted in its foul devastation, the abode of "every unclean and hateful bird." Thus should it be with the horrid desolation of the papacy. With this one dreadful, ghostly, picture, is the double fall of the papal church spread before our eyes. This event finds a place in the prophetic abridgment of Ecclesiastical history in the 14th chapter; and again is it announced, but now more fully.

We come now to the *reasons* for this overthrow. Her connection with the "nations" by which these had come to be partakers of the penalties of her fornications; her unlawful association with the "kings of the earth;" and the manner of her support of the merchants of the world, who "are waxed rich through the abundance of her delicacies," or the power and influence of her pride and arrogance—veritable things in those days when her patronage was extended to her merchants, and when traffic with heretics was forbidden: these, enter into the causes of her destruction. The wealth of countries under her dictation was granted to her allies, and worldly profits were reaped from connection with her; while the nature of the fornications of "kings" with her, and the effect of her association with "nations," have already been indicated.

Amid the symbols and declarations, as we often

find, is an interlude sounding from heaven in appeal to the people. If we will say that "there are some good people in the Catholic church;" and if we judge that there are many true Christians in that church which is in some respects a part of the other—the "Episcopal" church, Protestant greatly in name; then comes to these "another voice from heaven, saying, Come out of her, my people, that ye be not partakers of her sins, and that ye receive not of her plagues."

"For"—and here we find another reason for its destruction—"her sins have reached unto heaven, and God hath remembered her iniquities." It is not exceptional evil and general goodness that is here displayed; but a vast predominance of iniquity: "her sins have *reached unto heaven*"—as piled mountain high, and they demand retributive notice from the great God. Look at papal Rome in its chief representative men, and what do we behold?—a succession of men, for the most part, pure and good? Not so, but a line of men who on the whole have been more wicked than any other class; men guilty of bloodshed, of idolatry, of immorality, of incest, of lasciviousness, of monstrous forms of vice; some taken in the very act of adultery. One of the Pope's licensed brothels in Rome. A Roman Catholic historian says of Pope Alexander VI., that he was 'one of the greatest and most horrible monsters in nature that could scandalize the holy chair. His beastly morals, his immense ambition, his insatiable avarice, his detestable cruelty, his furious lusts, and his monstrous incest with his daughter Lucretia, are at large described,' 'by authentic papal historians.' Writing of the Popes generally a Roman Catholic declares: 'The chair of St. Peter was unsurped rather than possessed by monsters of wickedness, ambition, and bribery. They left no wickedness unpracticed.' This is the kind of men who are now pronounced to have been infallible; for the Decree of Infallibility is retrospective, as well as prospective. Read the historical accounts of examinations into the condition and practices of the Religious Houses in the sixteenth century; and you see an amount of iniquity that appalls you —iniquity, permitted and sanctioned by the papal church; bishops and priests being allowed to keep their mistresses. Look into the wine cellars of priests now; note that baskets of champagne are voted for at Catholic Fairs; consider the conduct of the mass of the communicants of the Romish church, the majority of whom are given to profanity and intemperance and sabbath-breaking; and you have some idea of the "cup of abominations" which Revelation declares to be "full" of sins that reach "unto heaven."

She has "glorified herself"—how much! She has lived "deliciously"—riotously, and "saith in her heart I sit a queen, and am no widow, and shall see no sorrow." She has so done and said, and declares this still. Notwithstanding she has been bereft of the kings of the earth, she asserts that she is not a widow; and in the end "shall see no sorrow;" which language is almost precisely the same as that which Roman Catholic writers affirm the Pope now uses as they visit him with words of condolence.

For these things: and for her traffic in earthly goods; selling the pardon of sin for money, and worldly treasures, for jewels and clothing, for ornaments and building material—as to raise means for the building of St. Peter's—and for all things merchantable; and, withal, because of the persecution of God's true people, has she been deemed worthy by God to be destroyèd and "utterly burned with fire; for strong is the Lord God who judgeth her." As in "one day, death, mourning, and famine," shall overtake her.

The *effects* of her downfall are portrayed: the effects of this on those who have had friendly dealings with her—kings, and merchants, and seamen; rulers of the earth, business men, and those commercial powers, which were sustained by her, and which had the wealth of the new, as of the old world, at their command. The picture is of *all*, who, in all time, have been enriched by her—and not simply those living at the time of her overthrow— uprising to view her destruction, and beholding the sources of their wealth destroyed, and bitterly lamenting the great change. One must needs be a reader and student of history, if he would take in this view which embraces land and sea, rulers and subjects, during a long period of papal rule. But he who is such will have no difficulty in seeing that the end of papal Rome is that of a power which has been pre-eminently connected with traffic on land and ocean; that great maritime powers—such as France, Spain, and Portugal, have been tributary to Rome in days of their conquests and wealth. The very able American Editor of Lange on Revelation, whose notes are even more satisfactory than Lange's comments, writes of the commerce of Rome: "It should be remembered that in the days of the Apocalyptist, Rome was not only the centre of the Empire, but in a peculiar sense her boundaries were coterminus with those of the Empire; the commerce of the entire State was hers—at once resulting from and ministering to her wealth and power. A peculiar relation continued to be borne by the City to the nation dwelling within the pale of the old Empire, even after that Empire had been shattered into fragments. Even to the present day she is in a sense the capital of Papal Europe. And still further—the relation of Rome to the peoples of whom she was and is the acknowledged capital, well symbolizes the relation of the Visible Church to Christendom. She is its inspiring centre—the source, and to a large extent a partaker, of its power and splendor. The commerce of the world is, in a peculiar sense, hers. To Rome actual, and Rome symbolical (in the sense set forth,) the description of these verses is applicable.'

But, if those who have been enriched by her bewail her fall; not so, do God's true servants. Shall any say that the Popes are the successors of Peter and the apostles? Hear the word of the angel: "Rejoice over her, heaven, and holy apostles and prophets: for God hath avenged you on her." There is to be gladness among these over the downfall of that "Woman,"—that church, which has been really an enemy of apostles and prophets.

The *manner* of the final and retributive destruction, is pictured. Already has it been declared that "her plagues shall come in one day," one "year," or "one hour" of the day and year—"death, mourning, and famine." Spiritual Rome shall be thus wasted, stripped, "and she shall be utterly burned with fire," as it is afterward set forth in chapter 19: 20. Some predict a literal fulfillment of the symbol in the destruction of Rome, and form their judgment upon the volcanic nature of Italy. Whether this is intended or not, the end shall be real and sure. Violently, suddenly, forever, shall she be cast down, "and shall be found no more at all." "A mighty angel took up a stone like a great millstone, and cast it into the sea, saying, Thus with violence shall that great city Babylon be thrown down." In the 19th chapter that sea is pictured as a "lake of fire and brimstone."

The papacy is now centered in the Pope, is embodied in him. Romish councils are virtually done away with; for the Vatican Decrees declare: "That in all causes, the decision of which belongs to the church, recourse may be had to his (the Pope's) tribunal, and that none may re-open the judgment of the Apostolic See, than whose authority there is no greater, nor can any lawfully review its judgment. Wherefore they err from the right course who assert that it is lawful to appeal from the judgments of the Roman Pontiffs to an œcumenical Council, as to any authority higher than that of the Roman Pontiff." Any who even say to the contrary of this decree are accursed: "Let him be anathema," is the sentence. The "definitions of the Roman Pontiff are irreformable of themselves, and not from the consent of the church"—these, are among the last words of the Vactican Decrees. The impious assumption of Infallibility, which is intended as a source of strength, shall prove to be an element of weakness and decay; for, as, in the providence of God, the Pope and Popedom are set aside, the Romish church itself, divided and weakened, shall crumble away; as this pretended " rock " sinks, the building raised upon it shall, likewise, go down into the depth of the sea; neither the one nor the other being able to uplift itself, any more than could a stone rise of its own power from the bed to the surface of the ocean.

The thought is sometimes entertained that the Pope, crowded out of Rome permanently, may be induced to move to some other place—possibly, to America. But the papacy is committed against this. To maintain such a thing is condemned in the Papal Syllabus of Errors, the 35th of which pronounces against "transferring the pontifical sovereignty from the Bishop and City of Rome to some other bishopric and some other city."

In that city has it decreed to abide; and Revelation links the Babylon-woman, even in its fall, with Rome. Undesignedly shall men carry out the prophecies of God's word.

This destruction of papal Rome is to be *final*. "And the voice of harpers, and musicians, and of pipers, and of trumpets, shall be heard no more at all in thee; and no craftsman, of whatsoever craft he be, shall be found any more in thee; and the sound of a mill-stone shall be heard no more at all in thee; and the light of a candle shall shine no more at all in thee; and the voice of the bridegroom and of the bride shall be heard no more at all in thee; for thy merchants were the great men of the earth; for by thy sorceries were all nations deceived." So, is stilled the merriment of her festivals, and the sound of her ceremonies, and all her activities; and the light of the candle goes out on her altars, and she becomes ecclesiastically as she is now temporally, extinct,—extinct so far as earth is concerned; but terrible, the retributions of the future world in store for her.

This remains to be carried out; but that it shall come to pass is just as sure as the fulfillment of the symbols which foreshadowed the destruction of her temporal power. I have shown you, I trust, satisfactorily, that the pictures of the Babylon woman have reference to the coming end of that vast ecclesiasticism which has cursed the nations and the world for hundreds of years.

One thing appears very prominently from a consideration of the subject of this lecture; viz., that an ecclesiasticism however vast, however strong, however sustained; though sitting upon the seven-hilled city and receiving strength from all the kingdoms of the earth; and though robed in richest attire, even clothed with the wealth of the world; and notwithstanding as a great city it should be triumphant over those whom it looked upon as its enemies, being drunken with the blood of these;—that such is not necessarily right, and may be in the end, weak: "For strong is the Lord God that judgeth her," who can in his providence overthrow and consume it, and by all means at his command make it to be "no more."

We learn, that however great the favor which an organization may have in the eyes of men, of even the kings of the earth; and though it dazzle human sight with its brilliance, and awe the human mind by the greatness of its power, God looks through the outward pomp and power at the heart, and only a right moral condition avails before him. The thing may claim to be of him; it may call itself Christian; it may, in its self-glorying, name itself the "only true church," and hold its earthly head to be infallible: yet God will not spare it for all this, but will visit it for its sins and abominations. It is only character—not wealth, nor power, nor magnificence, nor even creeds, which answers before him. This is a lesson to all professed churches and Christians. We may build our grand church edifices, and gather wealth in our membership; and all may seem fair and be imposing, yet this shall be no shield against his righteous indignation, if evils are practiced and sanctioned within, are cherished even in the heart.

No more striking comment could be made upon the words of Jesus, "My kingdom is not of this world," than the history of papal Rome and its predicted and partly accomplished downfall, affords. It is a fearful warning against the political union of Church and State. Not even the true churches of Christ need this, and would be harmed by it; and, in turn, being corrupted by such union—would injure the State. It is not thus that Jesus meant the "kingdoms of this world" should become his kingdom; for this is to be brought about, as we saw in connection with the sounding of the Seventh Trumpet, by moral means, in the triumph of the principles of a true Christianity.

There is a warning against greed for wealth, against intolerance, against self-seeking; and a lesson that above all, and, if needs be, to the exclusion of every other consideration, we seek to be right before God. We might personally have wealth as great as that ever controlled by the Romish church; we might be exalted in honor among the kings of the earth, and by these; we might wield a mighty influence over the multitudes and peoples of the earth; but all should avail nothing, if we were not right "before him with whom we have to do." If you are right before him it matters not, if all the world looks upon you as wrong; if you are wrong before him, it signifies nothing though all men believe you to be right. You *are* wrong before him, if you are an impenitent sinner. Though you may have committed no crimes against man, you are still a criminal in God's sight; for you have broken his great law of love—of supreme love to him, and complete love to man. Call, then, upon the sin-pardoning God for mercy! Look by faith to the cross of Christ, and be saved! True must be our faith in him. Not devotion to the mere name of Christ, or sign of the Cross, will suffice; for multitudes have had this "form of godliness" who in their lives have "denied the power" of true righteousness. God grant that our faith may be scriptural, and be the product of his spirit; thus, saving and abiding, manifesting itself in grateful and loving service rendered freely to him.

IX.

The Great Conflict.

Revelation, Chapter 19.

IF—as I firmly and fully believe—the symbols of Revelation are indeed Divine Pictures of the Christian Centuries, then we might properly look among these for some portraiture of the Present. But we are to take the pictures in our hands, in the order of their presentation, as we carefully and earnestly search for the originals—seen by the divine mind before these came forth to human view.

So doing, we shall not fail to see rising all about us events, which, shaped in allegory, will find themselves mirrored in the 19th chapter of Revelation. If the interpretations already given are correct, we are naturally brought now to pictures of the Present and immediate future. By a comparison of the scenes now depicted with the closing symbol and declarations of the 11th chapter, with the visions of the 14th chapter—those prophetic summaries of history—and with the 16th chapter, from verse 13 to 16, which had reference to the future; we shall be able to connect what is now to come before us with the sounding of the Seventh Trumpet, which has just commenced, and which covers the next great period of the world, continuing to the Millennium.

Added, then, to the interest growing out of the fulfillment of many of the symbols we have viewed; added to the bearing of past history upon us, "upon whom the ends of the world are come"—which may be said more forcibly now than in the days of the Apostles, is the interest of our being actors on the arena of now opening events. The pictures have now to do with us. We are at least on the skirmish line, on the outposts of those forces which are to meet in a conflict that is to decide the world's long peace and rest; if not the final combat of the great campaign of human history, yet only next to this.

The end of the battle is placed beyond a doubt even at the beginning. In our last lecture we noticed the prophecy of the utter ruin of one of the greatest enemies of true Christianity and of the welfare of the world. The strife which closes with the rout of this foe is next given. The certainty of triumph was understood in heaven, for the conflict is *preceded with the shout of victory.* As when contending armies come together, it is with loud cries, especially on the part of those hopeful of success, and more especially if they see that the battle is to go well for them; so do we hear heaven ring with the notes of anticipated triumph. As the symbol of Babylon cast as a stone into the sea, never to come forth again, was exhibited, "John heard a great voice of much people in heaven, saying, Alleluia." It was a special cry, for this is the only place in all the New Testament where this term is used. "Alleluia"—"praise Jehovah!" was the shout; "salvation, and glory, and honor, and power, unto the Lord our God; for true and righteous are his judgments: for he hath judged the great whore, which did corrupt the earth with her fornication, and hath avenged the blood of his servants at her hand." One glad outcry was not enough. The word burst forth again from full and jubilant hearts: "Again they said Alleluia." "And her smoke rose up forever and ever." "And the four and twenty elders and the four beasts fell down and worshipped God that sat on the throne, saying, Amen; Alleluia." The representatives of the church in heaven joined the cry of victorious praise. All God's servants, all that feared him, "both small and great," young and old, were called upon to praise him; and as with the "voice of many waters, and as the voice of mighty thunderings," did they answer, "Alleluia! for the Lord God omnipotent reigneth." Earth and heaven mingle the notes of adoration to Jehovah. All the glory of the triumph was given to him even before this took place, as it should be afterward, and forever.

Heaven recognized that the coming victory meant the complete union of Christ with his church, that the marriage supper was now to occur; for "his wife hath made herself ready," to be presented to her husband. Though the marriage-vow had already been pronounced, the bride had not been led to the home of her spouse to abide with him continually; and the supper which was to go before even this was now to be enjoyed. The theoretical, the mystic union; or, the union spoken of graciously and prophetically before the realization, was to become practical. It was to be accomplished in the actual condition of the church. This should appear arrayed in fine linen, clean and white; and "the fine linen is the righteousness of the saints," which should be "given them;" and they should be made personally "righteous as he is righteous." The grand idea is, that the coming triumph in the Great Conflict is to embrace the perfection of God's people, when no longer—as now—the church of Christ shall be reproached becaused clothed in garbs of worldliness, or with garments even "spotted with the world;" but shall be seen and recognized as "white and clean." The righteousness should be theirs by impartation as by imputation. Christ's righteousness shall be actually worn as a robe, not only to shield from danger, but to be fully and in every sense possible possessed. "Blessed," indeed, "they which are called unto the marriage supper of the Lamb." "Let us be glad and rejoice, and give honor to Him," whose reign shall involve the true and complete harmony of his church with his Son, "the Lamb of God who taketh away the sin of the world," and unto whom we shall be presented without spot, or wrinkle, or any such thing.

The Apostle who has communicated to us all the great Revelations made to him, does not say much about his own feelings. Now and then a glimpse of him is afforded, and we see that his mind and heart were greatly affected. As did he lose sight of himself, so do we almost forget him—as we well may—amid such great disclosures of human history. But, in connection with the present vision, he gives us in a word a view of the emotions which possessed his soul. In view of all he had seen, as the end was being brought so gloriously near, and the triumph of Christ and his church was assured, he was overwhelmed with the spirit of grateful worship. He felt to respond to the call: "Praise our God, all ye his servants." Have you not thus felt? Has not your mind glowed as with the light of the coming glory of the Lord and his cause on earth? Have you not said, again and again, "Thank God" for these grand realities, for the sure hope of victory? Did John see the symbols and feel to worship? So do we look at the same Divine Pictures, and we are inspired to adore God with renewed fervor. He fell at the feet of the angel to worship him, but the angel said: "See thou do it not: I am a fellow-servant of thee and of thy brethren who have the testimony of Jesus; *worship God*. For the testimony of Jesus is the spirit of prophecy." The angel who served John as he showed unto him these things, serves us, also, by these; and in these we have the "testimony of Jesus," "the spirit of prophecy."

The confident shout of heaven, whose spirit the Apostle caught, was followed by *a vision of the embattled hosts*.

First is seen the army of heaven, the forces of good. The great *leader* is at the head of these, and is the most prominent personage of all. How we stood in the old army days, and watched the troops pass by! There were Generals of note; there were corps, and divisions, and regiments, of fame; there were colors, honored, because battle-torn; but the object of chief attention was the commanding officer of all. So, the great commander of the moral forces of good is seen riding forth at the head of the column—the greatest and grandest of all. Be it remembered that we are still dealing with symbols; and, while these stand for realities, they but represent these. While, then, we behold here, without doubt, a vision of the Lord Jesus Christ, it is not of him in a personal, bodily form that should be visible to our eyes; but, like that other time when he rode forth "from conquering to conquer," so now does he appear in a moral conquest. Again he rides upon a "white horse," emblem of innocence and victory. I see nothing in this to give the idea of his second advent in bodily form.

What glorious *names* he bears, expresive of his character and warfare. He was "called Faithful and True, and in righteousness he doth judge and make war." He is faithful to all his prophecies and promises, true to his people; and only by righteous means and for righteous reasons, does he engage in a war that shall end in the triumph of righteousness. "His name is called, The Word of God," a name which we cannot understand; for it is the exponent of God himself, of whom Christ is the expression and embodiment. "And he hath on his vesture and on his thigh a name written, King of Kings and Lord of Lords." Thus, in his threefold name, are his relations to his people, his character, and his position, denoted. In all these does he assume command in the Great Conflict. "His eyes were as a flame of fire," as we have before seen, enabling him to observe all things, to overlook all the battle-field, and to behold all his enemies—however concealed, however subtle—just who and what these are, reading the hearts of all as readily as outward forms. "On his head were many crowns," won in engagements up to this time. "And he was clothed with a vesture dipped in blood," as did the prophet Isaiah behold him come "with dyed garments from Bozrah." There was a double significance, there as here. The blood of his enemies was sprinkled upon his garments, and stained all his raiment, as he trod the wine-press; yet was he in all this apparel "mighty to save," to aid. He is robed "with a vesture dipped in blood"—in the blood of atonement; for he is thus manifest before "he treadeth the wine-press of the fierceness and wrath of Almighty God."

But mark the *weapons* of his warfare. They are "not carnal, but mighty through God." "Out of his mouth goeth a *sharp sword*, that with it he should smite the nations." This is his great weapon; and to interpret this otherwise than as being the *word of God,* would be out of harmony with previous Scriptures. This is the sharp two-edged sword of the spirit, the rod of iron with which he should rule the nations. It is by his truth, his word,—not by the simple letter alone, but by all which this expresses,—by the principles of this, wielded in a special manner, and by his very hand, or as by his own mouth, that the combat is to progress. This is the instrument which Christ is employing now, and which he is to use in the future more fully than in all the past. The nations are to come under its power as never before; not only under its doctrines mentally—which latter have been thus received at times by whole nations and been perverted into occasions of carnal strife; but under its heart-subduing force, when it shall "rule" men truly, forcibly, firmly.

The *armies of heaven* are to follow him "upon white horses, clothed in fine linen white and clean;" which garb as we have already noted, "is the righteousness of the saints." They are to follow Christ readily, as upon horses; in innocence, and are to be clothed with true righteousness. No weapons are in their hands; they but aid that one sword proceeding out of the mouth of Christ. They are empty handed so far as mere human means are concerned; and their power seems to reside *in their robes*, precious as "fine linen, white and clean." Need I interpret this?—to say how we are to war, as here taught?—how we may hope to accomplish anything, and contribute to the triumph of Christ's cause? You will see that it is simply by *following Christ and the divine sword;* that it is by our *lives*,—a godly, righteous, saintly, Christian life, we are to press forward the conquests of Christ and the subjugation of the world to him. Nothing is said of even the words of God's people. These do not appear to form our great weapon in the conflict; these are naught beside the garment of righteousness clothing our nature and our deeds. This is not saying that we are not to preach and teach, and seek to persuade men to be reconciled to God; but, as our words favor the sharp sword of divine truth, so our lives are to give momentum to our speech.

This I believe to be the plain, direct, positive, teaching of this part of Revelation. I am not unmindful of other interpretations of the marshaling of Christ's army, nevertheless I think that this is right and that they are wrong; that Christ is not represented as going forth to the retributive judgment of the world, but in that strife which shall end in the overthrow of the enemies of his cause and shall usher in the Millennial glory; the final Judgment and the punishment of the wicked succeeding this. The armies of heaven are not formed of the angels; the saints are his consecrated people on earth, who had part in that other "war in heaven," or the moral world, sketched in a former part of the symbols. This will be disclosed more fully as we progress in the lecture.

With this view of Christ and his army, so arrayed, spread before the heavens, an observing angel is seen standing as "in the sun"—in the very sunlight of the eternal Father's countenance which shone with its vision over the entire scene of conflict; standing, as before the great Ruler of the universe, and viewing all things in his light—in the light of God; and he "cried with a loud voice," in full assurance of the result, even before the battle was fought, as to "all the fowls that fly in the midst of heaven, Come and gather yourselves together unto the supper of the great God; that ye may eat the flesh of kings, and the flesh of captains, and the flesh of mighty men, and the flesh of horses, and them that sit on them, and the flesh of all, free and bond, both small and great." Without distinction all were to be subdued, and their subjugation would constitute the feast, "the supper of the great God." The joy, the satisfaction of the triumph, would be to the soul as a feast to the body.

Now appear on the scene—creeping forth, combining, pressing forward, the *hordes of evil*. "And I saw the beast, and the kings of the earth, and their armies, gathered together to make war against him that sat on the horse, and against his army." You have only to turn to the sixteenth chapter, 13–16 verses, referring doubtless to this combat, to complete this picture. These, then, are the battalions. They are *spiritual;* and they represent satan in Paganism, papal Rome, and the false Prophet. They are a combination of these evil powers; and they gather "the kings of the earth, and of the whole world, to the battle of that great day of God Almighty;" that is, they gather the Nationalities to this. The host is made up of every-

thing opposed to Christ and his true people; and
"with signs and lying wonders" are they to work:
"for they are the spirits of devils working miracles."
Their weapons are deceit, error, and evil principle.
The whole picture is of nations, in their representatives, gathered together; and by all possible means
of delusion, they are to war against Christ and his
true cause on earth.

The contest is really Christ's, and, with him, are
his people; as against satan, and Rome, and false
prophets. There is mingled aggressiveness and
defense on the part of the former; they should be
assailed, but they should follow up their victories.

We look to see the Conflict; but, lo! *it is not
pictured,*—it is an unseen strife. No symbol of it
is given; as if it was inward, not outward, nor such
as could be expressed in outward forms. It is one
of principle, a great moral warfare; not such as we
have hitherto seen among the nations—those bloody
strifes of arms, but of the truth against error, of
right against wrong, of liberty against oppression,
of light against darkness; and the "kingdom of
God" is to come "without observation," for it is
"within us."

Remembering the order of the Apocalypse: that the Great Conflict was to follow the Seven Last Plagues, which have now finished their work; and that the conflict is to have bearing upon the second or double fall of Babylon, of Rome purely as a church, and you learn the warfare to be, as I have already declared, that upon which we are entered, and which is next before the world. The "beast" still "is," as the Babylon-woman, and the false prophet is yet in the world; the "unclean spirits" are abroad: papal Rome, the spirit of Slavery, and Spiritism, with all their kindred evils, are defiant; and in some form the battle is to be waged, to be— how fierce, we know not; yet, seemingly, is to be unattended hereafter with material weapons,—at least, no symbol is given of such encounters as have been pictured and realized in the past, except in that early strife in the moral world.

It may be a war involving modes of education; and be, also, social and political in its nature. Great questions of mind, of home, of civil rights, may enter into it; certainly, it is to be a combat of truth against error, of the Bible against all forms of evil and unbelief. That such a strife is before us, in which the "Beast" in the form of the Babylon-woman is to be arrayed against Christ and his true people; in which the subject of equal human rights is to be agitated (for the late war in our land, it now seems, has not fully decided this, despite the earnest efforts of the lamented Sumner—to say nothing of the bearings of the question upon other lands); in which Spiritism, and Mormonism, and every false prophet, are to have part; in which science is to be made to cross blades with the sword which proceedeth out of the mouth of the Lord Jesus Christ;—that such a conflict is at hand, Revelation indicates and our eyes do plainly behold, in the arming and mustering of the forces. We know that these do exist—active, full of purpose, and malignant, on the one hand; strong, and able in equipment and leadership, on the other, the great Captain of our salvation calling the armies of heaven, his people, to his "help against the mighty."

He is blind, or blind-folded by earthly cares and concerns who does not see the lines of battle—line upon line of the army led by the Dragon against Christ and his forces. Even the friends of the Babylon-power recognize that the strife is upon us.

Archbishop Manning, thought to be by far the ablest as he is the most distinguished Roman Catholic prelate in the United Kingdom, has declared in the progress of his discussion with Mr. Gladstone, that "the world is on the eve of the mightiest religious controversy it has ever witnessed, at least within the last three hundred years." A Catholic paper speaking of the debate, says: "The first guns have been fired in this 'great religious strife.' We await the next." The words of Archbishop Manning are not those of one who merely notes, however interestedly, the signs of the times; they are the utterance of one who is in the secret counsels of the Pope, who has been rewarded for past services with the highest position his church can grant him in England, and who, doubtless, knows the purposes formed, the campaign mapped out which is to be prosecuted in Europe and America,—for never did General or Council of War more carefully mature plans of operation than does the papacy. "Wise as serpents, and as harmless"—as these, are its ecclesiastics.

The apprehension of this struggle exists in our country, there being even fears of a religious war.

Already there are mutterings of a strife of the principles at issue. This has commenced in the press, and at the ballot-box; and it is to assume an intensity scarcely imagined by us now. Think we that the claim of the Pope, ratified by his minions in council assembled, to the supreme obedience of his subjects, does not extend to America? As—appealing to the enslaved consciences of these, he identifies allegiance to God with obedience to his own behests, may he not pretend to absolve Catholics from fidelity to this Government, as—so often before—he has again done, in Europe; this time, in Austria—where the recent liberal enactments establishing liberty of all "opinions, liberty of the press, and liberty of faith," were thus met by him? The Pope is the pronounced enemy of the "liberty of the press, liberty of conscience and of worship," and "liberty of speech;" he is the avowed advocate of the use of "force" in executing the behests of his church, the positive claimant to arbitrate even in civil affairs, clinging still to the temporal power of the Popedom. He is the declared foe of secular education, of our common schools; of everything, but his own selfish, greedy Babylon-power.

He is more intent upon regaining his lost earthly crown than upon possessing a crown in heaven; more anxious for the worldly aggrandizement of his false church, than for the true salvation of men. If he will favor any means to gain his ends in Europe, let us see to it that he does not succeed in his efforts in America; nor organize his people into a fierce mob, and hurl them against the life of the Republic. Dr. Döllinger says: "By the new decree it is the duty of every layman, whenever it is intimated to him that this or that question has been decided by the Pope, to obey. When the Pope orders a man to vote in a specified manner, he is obliged, even in his capacity as a member of Parliament, to obey. That was never said before. *It is a new situation since 1870.* Mr. Gladstone brings this truth out in his pamphlet. He says that the civil elections of every Catholic country are now quite uncertain, because they depend entirely upon the will of a foreign potentate. This is the side of the question which ought to be studied in the United States too."

In the direct connection of the scripture, no particular *place* where the conflict should be waged, is stated or symbolized; as if this was to be general —over the world. But in the sixteenth chapter, where, doubtless, this same war is foretold, a place is specified; showing that while the war is to reach world-wide, there should be a most marked scene of strife—where the forces should be concentrated, and the blows struck which should be decisive of the whole campaign; the issue here, determining the struggle, and leading to the laying down of every hostile weapon. That place "is called in the Hebrew tongue Armageddon," which I have demonstrated to be a most apt figure of America. The kings, or nationalities of the earth, should be gathered together to "the battle of that great day of God Almighty." This gathering should take place peculiarly, so as to be noticed specially, as the waters of the Euphrates were being dried up, which latter we saw to commence about the year 1820. As a fact of history, it was in the year 1819 that for the first, by act of Congress, statistics of the number of Emigrants reaching this country were made. Since then, year by year, the record of the number has been kept; and that time nearly dates the rapid income of the mighty flood, hundreds of thousands of foreigners being borne in single years upon our shores, till the number has swelled to millions— poured from almost all nationalities into our cities, out on our prairies, far and wide. From the east and from the west they have come, and are coming. The Atlantic and Pacific waves bear up the tide upon our shores: papal Rome, largely on the one hand; pagan east, upon the other, are meeting here. The whole world, in its representatives, is coming together; and all are bringing their peculiar prejudices of nationality, of religion, of education; and the old conflicts of the ages are to be renewed in spirit, the great battle of all time is to be fought. A Catholic bishop, speaking of a recent visit to the Pope, says, that the latter " did not conceal the hope he felt of the growth of Catholicity in America and for its ultimate triumph in our prosperous country;" thus manifesting that the eyes of the Pope are turned toward this land as the scene of special effort. Thank God for the indirect promise of his word, that the strife is to be moral; for so shall it be, what conflicts of arms are not necessarily —truly and fully decisive.

You will own at least that this view of the scene

of the great battle nicely accommodates itself to the symbols; but I am not dealing with mere accommodations of truth; I am pointing you to the realization of symbols in facts, and if the other representations have met their counterpart in past history, so does the one before us find its fulfillment in a real order of things. I will not go over the reasons for this, but the interpretation must stand or fall upon the grounds given. I believe it to be true to the great principles of interpretation we have followed in the whole course of lectures.

On that old battle ground of Armageddon, among those great conflicts there waged, was one not decided by the numbers of the victors; but by the trueness and courage and devotion of each man, and the victory turned upon the battle cry of the conquerors: "The sword of the Lord and of Gideon!"—"For Jehovah and for Gideon!" This be our consecration, this be our inspiration—Christ and his true cause! The sword we follow, be the "sharp sword which goeth out of his mouth" "who is the Faithful and True, and who in righteousness doth judge and make war;" who is the "Word of God," the "King of Kings and Lord of Lords."

When the princes of Germany offered their swords to Luther to further the Reformation, he replied: "The *word* will do it." So, discarding material means, and looking beyond mere political triumph, let us rely upon the power of divine truth, most zealously used.

If the Great Conflict itself is not directly pictured, the *result* of this—like the forces engaged—is. "And the beast was taken, and with him the false prophet that wrought miracles before him, with which he deceived them that had received the mark of the beast, and them that worshiped his image. These both were cast alive into a lake of fire and brimstone." They were captured, and were cast as into a lake burning with sulphur; so, were punished and destroyed from the face of the earth. This is the picture of the *spiritual* overthrow of papal Rome and the false prophet; and of that punishment in reserve for the votaries of these. That it shall be fearful, is certain—as dreadful as a lake of burning fire to the body; that it shall be lasting, is sure, for "her smoke rose up forever and ever." That it involves conscious suffering, is taught; for they were cast into the lake "alive," and "they shall be tormented day and night forever and ever."

The victory shall be *complete*. All forms of evil and of error are to be subdued. Not only the beast and false prophet are to be destroyed—they in judgment and wrath; but "the remnant were slain with the sword of him that sat upon the horse, which proceeded out of his mouth; and all the fowls were filled with their flesh." The representation does not give us to believe that all shall be brought into loving subjection to the Lord Jesus Christ; but all shall be overpowered. Some shall be cast into the "lake of fire and brimstone;" others shall be vanquished with the sword of the spirit, with the sword of the Lord Jesus.

What a hopeful look the whole picture affords of the future immediately before us—before America and the world. How anxiously earnest minds are questioning as to the fate of our country,—whether civil liberty is to continue, or is simply a problem. The human outlook is not fully satisfactory. Our people are too greatly swayed by passion and prejudice, and too little by reason and principle; the commingling of elements is too varied; the friends of truth and right, too apathetic, and the votaries of error and wrong so active and determined, that the favorable solution of the question must come from a power above man, overruling all things for good. In the old world, the conflict is so largely one of material might, that—looking no further than the national features of it, the result seems doubtful. Yet be not faithless, but believing, O Christian, O lover of man; for the word of Jesus Christ points to the triumph of the Good and True: on the mountain heights of the future do we see, in the light of Revelation, the banners of Immanuel waving in victory.

Whatever the means Christ may use—and we are sure that "true and righteous are all his ways"— *our* duty is plain; we are to "follow the Lamb" whithersoever he leadeth, guided by that divine sword flashing before the eyes of our faith: we are to go forward clothed in that "fine linen, clean and white"—the righteousness of the "saints." We are to hope for the conquest of the world, and are to seek this now specially by means of our Christian character and devotion, only next to the word of God, or in connection with this.

The point we are to strike at is indicated. It is the *human soul*. This is the key of the position.

We are to touch men not outwardly, but by moral influence; not by material force, but by spiritual—by the power of divine truth and the influence of godly lives, brought to bear upon their consciences and hearts and wills. The present and eternal salvation of men is to be most earnestly sought. This is not only indicated as the line of our duty; but, oh! that this shall be done, that the gospel shall spread with renewed force to every land is pictured in that part of the 14th chapter which links itself with this very time: "And I saw another angel fly in the midst of heaven, having the everlasting gospel to preach unto them that dwell on the earth, and to every nation, and kindred, and tongue and people."

This great warfare is to take place as well on the battle-fields of *our own hearts*. Heaven saw that the casting of the beast and of the false prophet into the lake of fire should be connected with the "marriage supper of the Lamb." Through the conflict, or in this, the wife doth "make herself ready." Are we ready? Are we stripped of robes of worldliness? of worldly pride and self-seeking? of all evil? and are we clothed upon, in mind and soul, with garments clean and white? Do we feel all the evil forces working upon our own hearts? appealing to us—sometimes, how strongly! Do the beast and false prophet and satan himself assail us in our thoughts and in the desires and purposes, the motives and affections of our hearts—in our whole soul? Let us recognize in the assault a part of the Great Conflict. Every citadel is to be assailed; and every victory which every child of God gains in himself over these things contributes toward the grand result over which heaven and earth shall rejoice with singing. While we urge on as never before the triumphs of truth and righteousness in others, let us not be surprised ourselves and overthrown by the enemy; but, by as much as he holds any of the ground of our souls, be it ours, under the leadership of Christ and by the sanctifying might of his truth and spirit, to seek to dispossess the evil ones: so shall we best follow Christ to the conquest of the whole world.

I put a searching question to you all: Under whose standard are you serving? Who are you following? Which side are we aiding? "He that is not for us is against us," says Jesus. Are you for Christ? You cannot be neutral. Less and less shall men be able to be so. These great principles are defining themselves more and more, the lines of battle are becoming more and more distinct; and in the ranks of the one or the other are we found. The battle shall reach to every nation, to every home, to every heart.

I plead with you to-night for Christ. Because of love to him, and the desire to glorify him, I ask you to be for him. For your own good, I seek it. Choose the *right*: choose the Faithful and True one, the divine Jesus, the King of Kings and Lord of Lords. Choose the *victor* side; for we invite you not to defeat. Better to fall with the right than to stand with the wrong. But the right shall prevail. The sure word of prophecy declares this. In asking you to give your allegiance to Christ, I call you not to mourning and suffering; I joyfully, earnestly, in the name of my Master, bid you to a royal feast, to a marriage supper,—the marriage of the Lamb. "Blessed are they which are called unto the marriage supper of the Lamb." Aye, blessed such: blessed you who are called now; if you will "make your calling sure" by accepting in humble, penitent faith, the gracious invitation.

X.

The Millennium.

Revelation, Chapter 20.

YOU have seen the sun shining above the mountains in the west, and while the evening was coming on to you, you have understood that beyond the heights there should be sunlight still; and you have thought of the sunlit scenes on which your eye rested not. These were realities, you knew; and you knew that the same sun which had illumined your path and had shone around the world as this turned eastward, was to light up the things unseen by you, and to brighten all in glory.

Gazing from our present stand-point toward the heavens glowing with the symbols of Revelation, we behold the light reaching in advance of us—into the future, and shining upon realities yet to come, but upon realities as distinct as those of the past or the present. Heretofore, we have had greatly the advantage of events which have transpired to aid us in the interpretation of the Divine Pictures; we have been able, as we have judged what these naturally called for, to turn to history, or to look about us and ascertain if, in the past or present, there was anything which really corresponded with these; and we have not searched in vain. Though we have been surprised at the wondrous verification of the revelation of Jesus Christ, this has been only what we might have expected from a Divine Christ; his revelations placing themselves beside his miracles in confirmation of his divine nature and Messiahship. But now we must not only form an humble yet earnest opinion of what the portraitures mean, but of the things which shall probably answer to these; rather, we can only judge of their evident design, and must leave the realities to the great future.

Gladly, jubilantly, may we turn to the present Picture; for, if there has been doubt and there is still a division of sentiment as to some of the foreshadowings of the Millennium, there is no uncertainty as to the glory of this. All are agreed that it means morning to the world, that it shall bring the golden age to our race; that the grandest dreams of the possibilities of human nature on the earth, as it now is, are to be realized. As do Astronomers point us to the stars and tell us at best of only a few features of these—so distant are they; declaring that these are suns, giving to us some idea of the size and nature and color of these, and beyond this confessing ignorance; so do I direct you to the portion of Revelation before us now, indicating to you the lines of light and meaning, but not speaking with full certainty of the coming realities.

The term Millennium means simply a thousand years, and has come to be used in connection with the book of Revelation because of the "thousand years" here spoken of. It has in itself no other meaning, and in the scripture no other reference. It has no subtle significance. All of good associated with it has grown out of the symbols which clothe it in the Apocalypse, or has been based upon these.

Does it stand for a long, indefinite time? While, indeed, long, it would be contrary to the use of figures thus far in the book to say that this is the only meaning of the phrase. The time is definite.

If the years are prophetic, then they shall amount to 360 × 1,000 = 360,000 years. Some maintain that it is to be literally a thousand years. This, of course, would make an exception to a general rule. If you ask me, which is intended? I answer you: I do not know. I think that it is an exception, but I have no reason for this thought, except that 360,000 years would be very disproportionate to the other periods of the book, and to what we accept as the age of past human history. If it is to be literally a thousand years, then that mystic scripture number "seven" would be again in force, and the beginning of the Millennium might be looked for as 6,000 years of the world's history is completed. This would allow about one hundred and forty years more for the sounding of the Seventh Trumpet, and for the completion of the Great Conflict of principle on earth; and the Millennium would be the Sabbath-time of the race, its long and blessed period of rest. Whether this time be correct or not, that the Millennium shall be the world's Sabbath is true; and we shall scarcely find a better interpretation of the symbol than that of the Sabbath, God's design of this. We, then, should be at the Saturday-age of the world, with the earnest work of this on hand; with its busy and finishing toil engaging us, yet permitted to anticipate the speedy laying aside of its duties, and the coming on of rest, as "The world's long week is o'er."

In the Great Conflict which is to end in the overthrow of the Beast and False Prophet; indeed, of every error and evil which exalts itself against Christ and his cause, his people are to have part. Clothed in righteousness, and following the great Captain of God's host—riding forth with the sword of truth, we shall aid in securing the victory. One foe, however, shall remain after this—fierce, subtle, buffeting, warring—Satan. He is to be manifest not simply as the " dragon "—as embodied in the pagan power, or in the "beast;" but is represented in *all* his nature and character, as when he led in that conflict portrayed in the 12th chapter, and sought to destroy the truth and church of Christ. He is called "that *old* serpent;" as old as the temptation of man, and as old as his own apostasy from heaven. To his personal and universal subjugation *we* are not seen to contribute; but, says John: "I saw an *angel* come down from heaven, having the key of the bottomless pit and a great chain in his hand. And he laid hold on the dragon, that old serpent, which is the Devil and Satan, and bound him a thousand years." Such an one shall be required for the task. The chain shall be forged in heaven, and be formed of the power of God. With this, and not by human might, shall Satan be seized; and, being bound, shall be "cast into the bottomless pit, and shut up;" and the angel shall "set a seal upon him (or "it," the bottomless pit) that he should deceive the nations no more, till the thousand years are fulfilled, and after that he must be loosed a little season." Chained, imprisoned, with prison-house sealed as with the signet of God —by his authority, and none able to open the door, —this is the coming fate of the devil.

This, then, we do know about the Millennium, that satan's power shall cease from the earth during all that time; that by divine means and energy it shall be completely restrained. To understand all that this involves, were to comprehend the withdrawal of the secret source, the inspiration, the indwelling spirit, of the malignant power of paganism, popery, and the false prophet—the mainspring of all the cruel opposition, in word and deed, to Christ and his cause. To realize it, were to behold truly the taking away of the prime-mover in all the wickedness of the Jews, and of men in all ages and times, back to the betrayal of man in Eden. It means the arrest and imprisonment of the chief conspirator against the peace and good of men and the glory of God. If the head, the leader of organized crime is captured, all the band is broken and flees; and with satan's seizure, all his army of demons shall betake themselves into seclusion and inactivity. It would take more than human mind to grasp and human speech to express the condition which shall result from the fulfillment of this scripture.

As when some burning, consuming, blasting fire-fanned, fed, and fierce-winged in its dreadful sweep and flight, by the tempest, goes down and is extinguished, when the wind lulls and dies away; so shall the ravages of sin be checked as its burning fires are no longer excited and impelled by satanic power. As some deadly miasm—passing unseen through the streets, loading the air with death; entering the abodes of the people, when even the doors open not; stealing into the vitals—corrupting, withering, destroying; "walking in darkness and wasting at the noon-day," is mercifully removed and the air becomes pure,—as then, do fears and death pass away with the disease; thus shall it be when that subtle adversary and destroyer is curbed by the power of God, and his havocs are restrained upon earth. Words fail to do justice to that world-wide peace and blessing which are to come as the dreadful works of satan, pressed so earnestly through the ages, shall end, for at least a thousand years. Ah! thou "serpent," who hast crept with thy slimy folds and venomous sting into the world, and made of earth almost a hell; who hast glided among the fair flowers of our homes and left upon all the blight of thy trail; who hast penetrated human hearts with thy filth and fangs, and hast marred the image of God and made men to be like thyself; thou enemy, thy "destructions" shall cease! "The Lord rebuke thee," thou fell and foul deceiver and destroyer; as he shall bind thee, and, at last, punish thee through eternal ages. We will rejoice even now over the coming defeat of this adversary, and heaven itself shall ring with gladness because of it.

This is not saying that all men shall be true Christians then. Such a consummation is not declared in this connection; for there shall yet be a division in moral character on earth, since the world's people are at the end of the Millennium to be gathered against " the camp of the saints " and " the beloved city." But, though human nature may continue to be essentially the same, it shall not be backed by satanic influence, and aided as it now is, and has been, by the devil; and the people of God shall not be tempted and buffeted, assailed, and—if possible—deceived, through the power and wiles of the adversary. This shall make a vast difference in the world and to the church of Christ. If human depravity shall remain, this shall be unhelped by satan, and shall not oppose the church. The latter shall have free course in all its work, and its triumphs shall not give way to defeat. God's spirit shall not be hindered in his operations by the evil one, who now does his utmost to prevent revivals of religion, or to check these, or to destroy their fruits. This forms one feature of the Millennium—*satan shall not be upon the earth.*

As this is the most prominent peculiarity of the

negative side of the subject, so is there a prefigurement of the most notable positive phase of that Sabbath-age of the world. "And I saw thrones, and they sat upon them, and judgment was given unto them; and I saw the souls of them that were beheaded for the witness of Jesus, and for the word of God, and which had not worshiped the beast, neither his image, neither had received his mark upon their foreheads, or in their hands; and they lived and reigned with Christ a thousand years. But the rest of the dead lived not again, until the thousand years were finished. This is the first resurrection. Blessed and holy is he that hath part in the first resurrection: on such the second death hath no power, but they shall be priests of God and of Christ, and shall reign with him a thousand years."

The picture is chiefly that of a certain *class* of Christians, who in some sense shall exercise a special power for the time given. It accords with the tenor of other revelations, and displays the martyrs,—the class personified,—taken from before the altar of sacrifice, where they had been long waiting and crying—as it were—to God for deliverance, and thence exalted; their desire being granted, as God's people were raised above persecutions and henceforth virtually ruled upon earth,—were made " priests of God and of Christ," and " reigned with him a thousand years." The period shall, then, be one free from persecution; when the friends of truth shall no longer be subject to their enemies, and shall be unopposed in their adherence to the right. It shall be as if the martyrs lived again; for the representation is pictorial, and is limited to this one kind of Christians. It is not declared here that the Christian dead shall come forth from their graves; this is reserved until a later time, but the picture is of a *peculiar type of piety* which shall prevail upon the earth. The resurrection spoken of in this connection agrees with that coming to life of the slain witnesses portrayed in the 11th chapter; where, evidently, the intent was, that the *spirit* of the witnesses should live in the Reformers. John saw not the bodies of the martyrs, but their "souls;" he did not see the souls of all Christians, but only those of the Christian martyrs.

Some have thought that the beginning of the Millennium shall date the second coming of Christ in bodily form. But there is no symbol or assertion of this here. The Great Conflict we have viewed is moral; the triumph shall be spiritual. Satan, that great evil spirit, is to be bound; and the thrones, and those who sat down on these, present to view the conquering people of God in that strife which ushers in the Millennial glory, who, as representatives of God's triumphant cause, shall have supremacy through their moral power—the force of the truth and of personal godliness; while the "souls of those that were beheaded for the witness of Jesus and for the word of God" typify a spiritual condition. These live and reign as embodied in those who share their disposition; as a class, not as raised in body from the tomb. In view of all, we are not warranted in believing that this reign of Christ on the earth is to be a personal, bodily dominion. It would surely seem as if this would have been plainly delineated if it was to occur. We are prone to make the mistake which the Jews, and even the Apostles, long cherished, of associating an earthly crown with Christ; notwithstanding he has said: "My kingdom is not of this world."

The portrait, then, calls for a time when God's

people shall be distinguished by the *spirit of the martyrs ;* when, in this spirit they shall prevail, all men and all nations owning the power of their lives and words ; and, when it shall be recognized universally that Christ is " in them of a truth." " Seeing their boldness," all men shall confess, as they did of the Apostles, that "they have been with Jesus and have learned of him ; " and he shall reign in them and through them, and they with him. As he shall rule spiritually—for the "*nations*" shall continue in the four quarters of the earth; so the authority of his people shall be that of moral influence.

The coming age is to be characterized on the part of Christians [by those *elements* for which the Christian martyrs were noted, as much as if these were risen from the dead. These are celebrated for devotion to the *truth*. This shall be exalted in its purity, and be the governing power of faith and practice. There shall be no indifference to error nor compromise with this. God's people shall be seen to be guided by *principle*, by the true principles of his word ; above bodily emotion, subjecting even physical conditions to itself; and completely rejecting all mere *policy*. The latter, which has so large a place in the workings of Church as well as of State, of business and of social life, shall be a thing unknown in practice then. If men will justify themselves in this now, there shall be no need of it in that transparent period, when honesty of thought and purpose, and honest allegiance to the right, shall meet with a true response in all minds and hearts. "Sharp practice" and self-seeking shall be banished from the churches, and the Denominations shall find their true place, and be in honest, hearty sympathy and fellowship; the basis of all being the true word of God, and the bond—the reigning spirit of Christ. It shall be a time of true *adherence to* Christ, for his people shall rule with him in fullest accord. The spirit which led men to lay down their lives for his sake shall have a controlling power in the hearts of all his disciples. The great truths and principles for which the martyrs died shall be in the ascendant. So do we understand the picture.

"This is the first resurrection;" that is, this is the *nature* of the first resurrection; it is to be moral, spiritual, for only such is here portrayed according to the natural interpretation of the Divine Pictures. Only one other passage of scripture speaks of some rising first; 1 Thess. 4: 16: "The dead in Christ shall rise first." But, from the connection, the meaning is that the dead shall rise before the bodies of the saints, who are alive at the sounding of the last "trump of God," shall be changed. That part of 1 Cor. 15, which presents the truth of the resurrection of God's people, is not followed by a declaration that after this the wicked shall be raised; but it is said that "then cometh the end," all reference to the resurrection of the unjust being omitted, as the specific object was to comfort Christians in view of their own resurrection. Peculiarly "blessed and holy" shall they be who have part in the first resurrection; on such, indeed, "the second death hath no power"—that death the nature of which is afterward described.

It does not necessarily follow that none of the righteous shall die the natural death during the Millennial period. They, *as a class*, are to reign with Christ, but they are not made up of any certain *individuals* to whom is to be granted an antediluvian age; as if those persons who are alive at the commencement of the Millennium shall have an earthly existence of ten centuries. That God could make them live physically a thousand years, is true; but it is not a question of his power, so much as of the revelation of his purpose. Even now, as said Wesley: "God buries his workmen, but he carries on his work;" and, though during the Millennium his servants may die, Christ's reign in his people shall continue. The promise is not that the first death, but that the "second," shall have no power over them. It is only after the general resurrection that death shall be destroyed, and this is pictured further along, and is placed subsequent to the unloosing of Satan again, and after the promulgation of the fiats of the Judgment.

Here—in connection with the Millennium—comes in the passage which forms a part of that general, symbolic, summary of events given in the 14th chapter of Revelation and reaching forward to the spiritual fall of Babylon, to the long Sabbath of rest, and to the reaping time of the moral world: "Blessed are the dead which die in the Lord *from henceforth:* yea, saith the spirit, that they may rest from their labors; and their works do follow them." Dying, they leave not their "works," or sorrows through trial—the meaning here of the terms "labors" and "works"—upon the earth; these do follow them into the grave, for the true rendering of the scripture is, that these works do "follow *with* them." God's people now die, but the same trials they endure continue to live; not so, then. Physical suffering may be undergone and human anguish be felt, but spiritual trial shall not go forward as in the present. The idea that all pain and sorrow are to be absent is not given; this blessed experience is reserved for still another period, as indicated in the 21st and 22d chapters. But blessed, indeed, that time when Satan, whose ravages are worse than disease, shall be removed from the earth, and a Sabbath benediction shall rest upon the church and the world. Hasten ye hands of Time to lay hold of the mystic bells which shall chime in the glory of that blessed day of the Lord!

War shall then be unknown, and all human discord cease. We dig now, from old battle fields, weapons and missiles of past conflicts, and place them in our cabinets as curious relics of other and—it may be—

barbarous days; and we contrast them with modern implements of war, noting the improvement of firearms—the improved power and skill of destroying human life; but what an awful mark of progress and of advancing civilization! with only the compensating feature, that, because the means of destruction are more effective than heretofore, hostilities may sooner be ended. But in that coming age, armaments shall be practically unknown. As from old scenes of carnage—old then, familiar now— rusty rifle and cannon and sword, the bullet and broken-shell, are unearthed, these shall be both curiosities and matters of wonderment; the surprise being that man should ever, especially in times of boasted Christian civilization, have resorted to so cruel and unnatural a mode of redressing grievances or settling disputes as bloodshed, that the necessity for this should ever have been urged. "They shall beat their swords into ploughshares, and their spears into pruninghooks: nation shall not lift up sword against nation, neither shall they learn war any more. O house of Jacob, come ye, and let us walk in the light of the Lord," shall be the language of the people.

But even this long day of light and splendor is to have its evening. Human nature on the earth, unredeemed, is to ripen in its sinfulness toward a revolt against Christ and his church. Probably by a growing aversion to the blessings of peace even; chafing more and more against the truth; weary of the power of godliness—taught and lived—which restrained them, the nations are prepared for the coming forth once more of the arch-enemy of God and man. Oh! how he leaps in his black passion from the dark pit, and, with links of the chain yet clinging to him, speeds over the world; and, among those who are ready to do his bidding, practices his deceptive arts! The ungodly who have failed to repent, even under the unhindered blessings of the gospel; who could not even say: "The serpent beguiled me, and I did eat," now—utterly beyond hope—come beneath his power, and are organized into a mighty column, and are hurled in one desperate charge against the "camp of the saints" and the "beloved city." Only for a brief season does this last great battle continue. The assault is rolled back in confusion and utter disaster; for "fire came down from God out of heaven, and devoured them. And the devil that deceived them was cast into the lake of fire and brimstone, where the beast and the false prophet are, and shall be tormented day and night forever."

Now are given pictures of the Resurrection, of the Judgment, and of the Final Condition of impenitent, unsaved souls.

John "saw a great white throne," greater than all the thrones of earth; for it was the throne of the Ruler and Judge of the universe; white in its purity, and unspotted in its holiness and justice. He "saw him that sat on it, from whose face the earth and the heaven fled; and there was found no place for them." The vision is of the exalted glory of the Judge of all the earth, before the light of whose majesty all else is lost sight of, as the stars go out before the sun, rising in its splendor; so fleeing from sight. "And I saw the dead, small and great, stand before God: and the books were opened: and another book was opened, which is the book of life; and the dead were judged out of those things which were written in the books, according to their works. And the sea gave up the dead which were in it; and death and hell (or hades) delivered up the dead which were in them: and they were judged every man according to their works. And death and hell (or hades) were cast into the lake of fire. This is the second death. And whosoever was not found written in the book of life was cast into the lake of fire."

It is certain that this scene takes in the whole world in all the centuries. If we question about some of the words, there can be no doubt that the language exhibits all men, in all time, as now appearing before the judgment seat of Christ. Souls small and great stand before God, the souls of the dead as well as of those living on earth when the judgment day comes. Whether the persons had been buried in the sea, or, unburied, had withered and crumbled to dust under the power of death,—all, shall stand before God. Doubtless, all the New Testament teachings of the resurrection here come into force. The symbol is of the *universality* of the Judgment. All are made to appear in the presence of the great white throne; however or wherever they had died and been buried, or though unburied. It would seem from the double representation in the 12th and 13th verses as if Inspiration would guard us against the thought that the souls of the dead came from the grave; for death but yielded its power—as over God's saints; and the wicked, in "hades"—in the underworld, not in the grave (as Dr. Craven so ably and satisfactorily demonstrates in his Excursus on Hades, which forms one of the most valuable parts of Lange on Revelation,) came forth. Soul and body are embraced in this picture of the Resurrection and Judgment; this world—land and sea—delivering up the body, death surrendering its power; and the other world sending forth its occupants.

"The books were opened"—those great statutes by which the world shall be judged. The Judgment shall be "*out of those things which were written in the books, according to their works.*" The great volume of God's law and of his gospel—of his entire word—shall be unfolded; the book of Providence shall be spread forth; and, also, the book of conscience. These shall be the standards by which we shall be measured. If men will say: The Law of God was so searching we could not keep this, then shall they be convicted of sin because they believed not on Christ (John, 16: 9.) If they will plead that they had neither the one nor the other, then shall they be judged according "to the things that are made," which might have declared to them "the invisible things of God"—by the standard of God's goodness in nature and providence. Moreover, their own consciences shall be a law unto them. By these things, "according to their works"—not their creeds, shall men be judged. It shall then appear that the whole world has sinned, and this shall stand convicted by the lowest as well as highest rules of judgment. Certainly, justice shall be done by him who sits upon "the great white throne;" it shall be meted out to every person, for the ordeal shall be personal; we shall be tried as individuals, and not in the mass.

"*Another book* was opened." If all, as weighed in the divine balances, are found wanting; if all shall be unable to meet—with their "works"—the test of God's law, or to endure even the light of his goodness and of their own consciences, how shall any be saved? This shall be determined not by the good deeds we have done, offsetting the evil;

not by the plea that we have done as best we knew —for who has thus acted? who has not gone contrary to his own judgment of right; and, while approving the right in thought, principle, word and deed, practiced the wrong? The question on which shall turn our acquittal at the bar of God, in that great day, shall be: Are they "written in the book of life"—"the Lamb's book of life?" Have they become his by the renouncement of sin and self-righteousness, and by humble, true, heart-belief in the Lord Jesus Christ? in him as the Lamb of God who taketh away sin by the sacrifice of himself? It is faith in the atoning Savior, which, according to all the teachings of his word, secures a place for our name in the book of life. Even his justice shall unite with his mercy in favor of such; for the word is: "If we confess our sins he is faithful and *just* to forgive us our sins and cleanse us from all unrighteousness." The name truly inscribed in the book of life is the proof that the person has obeyed the *gospel;* and God, in covenant faithfulness, as in infinite grace, shall save. Perchance, the sins of God's people, forgiven and remembered no more by him, shall not appear at the Judgment; for they have "gone before unto judgment," and the only thing that may be determind, before the assembled universe, is, whether we are written in the Lamb's book of life.

Dreadful the punishment of the wicked, of the impenitent, the unsaved! If you will personify Death and the Under-world, and say that these, rather than their evil contents—which latter I believe to be intended—are to be cast into the lake of fire, which lake of fire is the second death; that death and hades are to give place to the second death, to Gehenna, which shall be the only death thereafter having power; yet, how fearful this! for it is the death that never relents, never dies: "Their worm dieth not and the fire is not quenched." "And whosoever was not found written in the book of life was cast into the lake of fire."

Doubtless, this is a symbol; yet what does it call for? For the most grievous realities, for an anguish as keen to the soul as a lake of fire to the body; moreover, for a fire that burns without destroying, which, with the tormented spirit, endures forever. As fire is energy connected with chemical synthesis;

so, the fires into which the impenitent shall be cast, shall be the violent, fierce, dreadful workings of sin upon the soul, the conscience and heart being burned with it forever and ever. Thus does the word of the loving God teach. Jesus announced pre-eminently—in love, we know—the awful truth; declaring it because it is a truth, and that we might be warned against the reality and be led, or driven, to seek safety in himself.

Think of the *company* among which the unsaved shall be hurled; aye, the impenitent from Christian lands, from Christian homes, from Christian sanctuaries—shall it be, also, false professors from Christian churches?—with names on church records but not "written in heaven?" "The *devil* that deceived them was cast into the lake of fire and brimstone, where the *beast* and *false prophet* are, and shall be tormented day and night forever and ever." All that is dreadful and distressing about "death" and "hades"—the present abode of the impenitent dead—shall be there; for these were, also, thrown into the lake of fire. Fearful symbol of justice! awful picture of the dread consequences and penalty of sin, and of impenitence and unbelief in Christ!

"This is the second death"—the suffering of the lake of fire.

Who would choose it? who, for the pleasures of sin for a season, would go to such a place, to dwell amid such horrid company—with a devil in torment, and with the quenchless fuel of sin to send forth its fiery arms to wrap about the soul forever and forever?

Yet such shall be your portion if you refuse or neglect to be placed in the Lamb's book of life. Do you not see, then, why we urge you to repent and believe on the Lord Jesus Christ? why, whatever gospel subject we bring before you, we come to this one point, Sabbath by Sabbath, "Believe on the Lord Jesus Christ, and thou shalt be saved?" "By the terrors of the Lord we persuade" you. Not that we always use these; but they are continually present to us, even when we plead his love with you. Oh! come to Christ by faith now! The Lamb's book of eternal life is open. He is ready to name you among the saved ones. Like Bunyan's warrior, who, with eye upon the Beautiful Palace, said to the keeper of the door: "Set down my name, sir!" and then pressed forward and strove to enter ; so, be it yours to pray, Set down my name, Lord! and then gird you for the Christian life and conflict, and urge your way onward in this, by divine help, toward the great white throne and the eternal life and glory beyond.

XI.
The Redeemed World and Glorified Church.

Revelation, Chapters 21, 22.

THE resplendent pictures of the last two chapters of Revelation need to be viewed beside the entire group of Divine Pictures, and to be studied in connection with the whole Bible. Whatever the things depicted, they are evidently those toward which the Patriarchs looked hopefully; for "they looked for a city that hath foundations, whose builder and maker is God." The vision of Prophets rested upon them, as they gazed through the mist and darkness of the ages relieved by the far off splendors of the city of God. Apostles were wont to say: "We, according to his promise, look for new heavens and a new earth, wherein dwelleth righteousness." To John was granted the the fuller vision of the coming glory; while we are permitted to take by faith a nearer view of this than all God's people gone before.

As the symbols of the Resurrection, the Judgment, and the last state of the wicked, were given, it remained in the wisdom and goodness of the Lord Jesus to spread before us portraitures luminous with the blessedness of the final condition of his people. Such do we now view in this closing lecture of our course.

The last chapters of Revelation have been long thought to present a picture of heaven as such; but I think you will conclude from a careful observation that this is not the primary, specific, thing described. The emblem is rather of the final surroundings and condition of the *church of Christ.* These shall, indeed, be heavenly; but the description is limited almost wholly of redeemed men The only representation of angels is where these appear as the guardians of the gates of the city. If the scene is heaven, it is so only in its relations to God's glorified people. Hence, I have chosen as the subject to-night, not Heaven; but the special things delineated—The Redeemed World and Glorified Church.

I. First, a *world* beaming with fresh beauty rolls before the vision of the soul. This new world is not necessarily another world than this; for afterward, when John was carried in spirit as to a "great and high mountain"—apparently of this world, he saw descending upon this the New Jerusalem. In the first five verses of the 21st chapter a *general* view is given; a symbol comprehending almost all that followed, shone forth. This indicates the future circumstances or abode of the church of Christ, fully "prepared as a bride adorned for her husband;" and reveals the condition of the whole world, which shall be occupied only by the saints.

What is that world? and, Where is it? are questions which shall always remain in doubt to the human mind, even to the minds of God's people, until the likeness shall be exchanged for the reality. That it shall be a definite world, is certain; for "earth," as well as "heaven," represents it. It appeared as "a new heaven *and a new earth*." Are we to understand that it is to be a world newly created? or, shall it be the present earth renovated, having passed through great changes which would fit it for human beings, also changed in their bodily conditions? and, is the great design of the symbol to present the idea of a new order of things? God speaking by the prophet Isaiah of "the new heavens and the new earth" which he should make, and which should "remain" before him, doubtless foretells a new condition of things on this earth; and the prophecy seems to be of the same glories pictured in the last Revelation. If this is the meaning of the scripture—that this earth is to pass through another transformation, as geologists affirm to be intimated by the present state of the globe, and so to be fitted for glorified men; then the strong language of the Apostle Peter, in his second Epistle, third chapter, declares not a complete destruction, but a great transition, and is, moreover, symbolical of an altered aspect of things morally; for to his mind the marked feature of "the new heavens and new earth" was, that therein should dwell "righteousness."

In harmony with this are the words of Paul: "For we know that the whole creation groaneth and travaileth in pain together until now." "The earnest expectation of the *creature* waiteth for the manifestation of the sons of God." "The creature itself shall be delivered from the bondage of corruption into the glorious liberty of the children of God:" our bodily natures shall be placed, at the resurrection, beyond the power of decay or death; and "we ourselves groan within ourselves waiting for the adoption; to wit, the redemption of our body." But more than this is true: the "*whole creation*" longs for that time, when it, too, shall be changed; when its mixed character of good and ill shall give place to only good; as with painful birth-cries does it await deliverance from its present state and its entrance upon a higher order of good. The earth, as it now exists, is eminently, in its very material workings, a world of probation and struggle, adapted to men in like moral as physical conditions; but the hope is given—at least intimated—that the very globe and universe shall be transformed into a theatre of only favoring forces, and, like the glorified bodies of God's people, be clothed upon with immortality. Just how the change may be effected, we know not; except, by the power of God, and, it may be, through the agency of fire—through new chemical combinations to which matter is, doubtless, susceptible. In what form the earth should then appear, we cannot tell, because this is not pictured; it is only disclosed that all the ill which mars it in the present shall be forever absent in that future and final state, and that the change shall be so great as to be virtually a new creation.

Astronomers reason that if there is intelligent life on some of the other planets of our solar system, it must be diverse in its material combinations from life here, owing to difference in the density of the worlds and their nearness to the sun, or remoteness from this. It were possible for human beings to be constituted otherwise than we are; and, moreover, for the human race to be so transfigured as to be adapted to a sea-less world, which is to be a characteristic of the "new heaven" and the "new earth." But that "there was no more sea" seen in this, may be symbolic only of the absence of all those things we associate in our minds with the ocean—uncertainty, instability, turmoil, division, among men, the world over. Now the sea occupies a large place in the economy of nature—useful now, not needed then; useful now, yet how uncertain, how treacherous, how dreadful!—surging between the nations and dividing human lives; sobbing ceaselessly on the shore, as if having part in the agony of human life; and tossed, oh, how fearfully, as in the mad strife of the world; and shrieking wild pæans over the wrecked whom it buries in the pitiless waters. But there shall be no sea in the new heavens and the new earth.

If it is true that in some form this earth is to continue, as the bodies of God's people, raised and transformed by his almighty power, are to become immortal like the soul; then a grander destiny is before matter than we have so far beheld. It certainly would appear as if this great and wondrous universe of worlds was formed for more than a transient mission, reaching through the few thousand years of human history and of man's apostasy; as if it might serve purposes extending to all eternity. With wisdom, and power, and goodness infinitely above our comprehension—though the conceptions we now have overwhelm us with wonder and delight—did God arrange this earth, through countless millions of years, to be the residence of man as he now is; and again could the Almighty change this world and re-adapt man, saved, to this. I am sure that the future and final abode of the redeemed, whatever it is or wherever it is, shall manifest God's glory as fully as this earth, more brightly than the heavens and earth as these now are; that it shall be worthy of God and most blessed to his people; the glory "revealed *in* us," be in harmony with the glory revealed *to* us, the one the reflection of the other.

There may be danger of too greatly literalizing these symbols; and we must bear in mind the scripture, having direct reference to the final form of the bodies of the saints, which declares that "flesh and blood cannot inherit the kingdom of God," that "this corruptible must put on incorruption, and this mortal put on immortality, and we all be changed" before we shall enter fully upon the new heaven and the earth. This transition shall be akin to that through which Christ's body passed as he ascended to heaven, and which spiritualization he could work at will when upon the earth. Certainly, that world shall be a *reality*; and though the earth which now is should not in any form enter into it, the gain should far outweigh the loss. If present material shall be transmitted, what we now see—

however glorious—is, in comparison with the other, only as the seed-corn beside the harvest, the bud in contrast with the blossom and ripened fruit; then, all those grand similes of the apostle, in 1 Cor.: 15th chapter, relating to the resurrected and immortalized body, would apply with equal force to the globe itself. If the terms "earth" and "heavens" are used as symbols only, they, at least, serve to exhibit a positive *place* as the final home of the redeemed, a place as real as this earth, and to which the "natural body" "raised a spiritual body" shall be conformed. I am not sure that we would not be satisfied without the forms of beauty which prevail here. How few look upon, or know anything about, or at all appreciate these, yet are they good people, even most earnest Christians; while we who know them, whose minds have been instructed about them, and who truly and fervently admire them, do not find full satisfaction in them; even here and now do we experience higher good and greater joy than are to be derived from them. We are not ready to fall down and worship the natural world; nor yet do we feel or believe that we could not be perfectly content and happy without this, especially in a world whose spiritual glories, though differing wholly from natural splendors of form, and line and color, of sky and clouds, of earth and mountains, of vegetation and water, should far exceed these.

There are two things positively set forth. The first is, that the new heavens and earth shall be *the peculiar and special abode of the glorified church of Christ*. Made ready for this, the church shall " come down from God out of heaven, adorned as a bride for her husband;" this, after the words have been spoken: "Come, ye blessed of my Father, inherit the kingdom prepared for you"—prepared in the purpose of God, as revealed by prophets and apostles, and the very words of Jesus—" from the foundation of the world." It is not said that the church goes up to heaven, but that it *"comes down from God out of heaven;"* the whole idea being of a special place arranged for God's people, and these made ready for that place, the one to be the counterpart of the other. That *"men"* are to occupy it, and that the "nations" still appear, represents an arrangement of glorified human life not wholly unforeshadowed now. All things are made new in character, but *the society* of the saints still remains society. The other thing is the holy and blessed *condition* of the new earth when possessed by God's people. "I heard a great voice out of heaven, saying, Behold the tabernacle of God is with men, and he will dwell with them, and they shall be his people, and God himself shall be with them, and be their God." This is Paradise more than regained; for God comes down to the renewed earth, here to make his tabernacle, here to "dwell"—not in types, not only in promises and ordinances; but "God *himself* shall be with them." All this is to be on the new earth, and is to be the universal experience of men, of his redeemed and glorified people.

As if to do away with the thoughts or fears which might arise, because the future home of his people is called an "earth," thus associating our present life experiences with it, the assurance is given that none of the trying features of our mortal existence shall be there known. For "God shall wipe away all tears from their eyes; and there shall be no more death, neither sorrow nor crying, neither shall there be any more pain; for the former things are passed away. And he that sat upon the throne said, Behold, I make all things new." Take these things from the earth,—take sorrow, and trial, and pain, and death, and with these, the curse of sin and the workings of Satan and all evil forces; and place in their stead an ever and fully present God, continually manifesting himself in the person of his dear Son, leading us to living fountains of water forever: and this earth, even as it now is, would be transformed into Eden, into heaven; for it is a wondrous earth, operated even by divine laws. Thus renovated, with the sundered bonds of life re-united, the loved Christian dead restored to us, we should be willing to live here eternally. But add to this such a changed constitution of the earth and of our natures—our physical nature, which is as much a part of us, as human beings, as our spiritual—as to free us from gross bodily conditions; and more than our loftiest imaginings have shaped would await us as the people of God; then, a world answering to all the promises and prophecies, and symbolic representations, would turn in its endless orbit about the throne of God.

Thus far has been given to us the sum and

substance of the closing and glorious symbols of the book of Revelation; for Jesus said: "Write; for these words are true and faithful. And he said unto me, *It is done*"—the thing is completed, the Revelation is virtually made, and the consummation of Time and of his grace has been pictured. "I am Alpha and Omega, the beginning and the end," who could speak authoritatively of these things; and who, abiding forever, shall bring them to pass.

Promise and warning are then pronounced: "He that overcometh shall *inherit all things*, and I will be his God, and he shall be my son." Shall we not seek to overcome our own evil natures, the world, and Satan? So, even by striving, by pressing forward in the Christian warfare? "All things" in the new heaven and the new earth; it may be, in the great universe of worlds, shall be within our reach; and the saints, with bodies "fashioned like unto Christ's glorious body"—independent of the laws of gravitation or even in harmony with these—may mount up into the heavens, as did Jesus in his glorified body, and move from world to world in his vast domains. This thought is justified by scenes in the life of Jesus,—by his transfigured glory, his walking upon the sea of Galilee, as well as by his ascension; and by the appearance of Moses and Elias upon the Mount of Transfiguration. The idea is sanctioned, by the manifestation of the angels of God upon the earth in the past. If any will doubt as to these things, none may question as to the exceeding glory and blessedness of the condition itself, whatever or wherever be the place portrayed. The inheritance of "all things" shall be as glorious as the infinite wisdom and power and love of the Lord God and his Christ can make it; it shall be the perfection of the expression of God's grace and love in Christ. For his sake, in reward of his work and worth, shall all this be ours as his humble disciples. Though "it does not yet appear what we shall be"—though we see nothing now which fully expresses it—"we know that when he shall appear we shall be like him; for we shall see him as he is;" and all our surroundings shall be in harmony with this exalted state.

"But the fearful, and unbelieving, and the abominable, and murderers, and whore-mongers, and sorcerers, and idolaters, and all liars, shall have their part in the lake which burneth with fire and brimstone: which is the second death." As dreadful the contrast with what has just gone before, as God and Satan, holiness and sin, reward and punishment, life and death; and all these things are true. If set forth, in great part, in pictures, these are less than the realities as the shadow is less than the substance.

II. It would seem as if a desire had sprung up in the heart of John to see by nearer view "the holy city, the New Jerusalem." Certainly, it pleased Jesus to grant this vision, and it may be, satisfy the desire. The Apostle had seen only the lines of light, and recognized that the object was the "bride of Christ." He says: "There came unto me one of the seven angels which had the seven vials full of the seven last plagues"—this one in particular, as if to keep before his mind that no other order of angels was to be sent forth—"and talked with me;" and as John, perhaps, expressed in the conversation his desire to see the holy city, the angel said: "Come hither, I will show thee the bride, the Lamb's wife. And he carried me away in the spirit to a great and high mountain, and showed me that great city, the holy Jerusalem, descending out of heaven from God." This is the second time that the description is given, but this is now followed by a more *particular* view of the thing portrayed.

I shall leave it for you to read, and re-read, the scripture words compact with meaning and glittering with beauty which delineate the city of God. I call your special attention to the fact that *the city is not a representation of heaven as such, but of the Glorified Church of Christ;* this simply, this only. The church is the Lamb's wife; she is "that great city, the holy Jerusalem" which cometh "down from God out of heaven, prepared as a bride adorned for her husband." This will afford you the key to that picture, which, next to vision of the Godhead, is the greatest and grandest of the Revelation, of the word of God.

Wondrous the magnificence of the church as she appears in apocalyptic robes, shining in light most precious; guarded as by "wall great and high" and by mighty angels, and thenceforth secure from all her foes; taking in all the tribes of Israel—the ancient people of God, the Jews, being brought in with the fullness of the Gentiles; comprising all Denominations of true Christians, who shall form the one city of God, the one bride of Christ. The gates of the city look toward all parts of the earth—east, north, south, and west. The walls are seen resting upon the "foundation of the apostles and prophets, Jesus Christ himself being the chief corner-stone;" and the foundation was "garnished with all manner of precious stones "— glistening with the truths taught by Apostles and Prophets and which now alone are fully seen in all their splendor; for the one thing peculiar to almost all the stones, is that this is the only mention of them in the New Testament, and, like the twelve precious stones on the high priest's breast-plate under the old Covenant, they reflect with the pureness of the highest product of the mineral world, the glory of God and of the Lamb, as they are brought to the light of his throne, as into the presence of the Shekinah.

The city appears complete, perfect : "The length and the breadth and the height of it are equal," for it has become as the Holy of Holies. It is a city of gold, since the church shall have been refined through all its trials, in all its furnaces of affliction, coming forth as pure gold. Although it has many gates, all are precisely the same, "each several gate was of one pearl;" so that the entrance is virtually one—Christ being forever the door of his church, the only entrance into his kingdom hereafter as into his spiritual church here. There was "no temple therein,"—no church edifice, no peculiar ecclesiastical organization; "for the Lord God Almighty and the Lamb are the temple of it." "The city had no need of the sun, neither of the moon to shine in it;" the church shall not need these lights. Now and in the past this appears "clothed with the sun, and the moon under her feet, and upon her head a crown of twelve stars." Truth expressed in word has needed to be a garment to her, and she has reflected the truth as from the moon beneath her feet, even giving birth to the truth; but, then "the glory of God doth lighten it and the Lamb is the light thereof." The personal presence of Christ shall do away with all need of what simply reflects him to us.

Mark the first five verses of the twenty-second chapter. They should not have been separated in any way from the preceding words; for they are one, and serve to blend heaven and earth in one.

By the repetition of some of the words, and the added symbols of "the river of water of life, clear as crystal," "the throne of God and of the Lamb," of the "tree of life in the midst of the street of it, and on either side of the river," bearing ceaselessly its fruits, the leaves being "for the healing of the nations"—of all the glorified nations of men who are akin to the church, to whom the doors of worship are always open—by these things, heaven and earth are united; and these figures give the assurance that the blessed and holy condition is to last forever.

Here is the water of life that gives eternal youth; here is the fruit of life never failing to nourish and satisfy the immortal nature; and no baneful influences shall ever prevail, for the leaves of the tree shall keep the air forever pure from withering, destroying ill. We shall not only live in endless health; but "there shall be no more curse"—no more sin, for "the throne of God and of the Lamb shall be in it;" and he shall prevent all evil by his ruling power, and we shall "reign forever and ever" over our sins and over the powers of darkness, for "there shall be no night there; and they need no candle, neither light of the sun; for the Lord God giveth them light."

All this is the picture of the Bride of Christ when she shall be presented to him, "not having spot or wrinkle, or any such thing;" but shall be "holy and without blemish." The city prefigures the church in its glorified state; the new heavens and new earth, its glorified residence. The former shall be forever open to God, whose light shall shine always upon it, and who shall dwell in his people and they in him. As did the Shekinah fill the temple of Solomon when this was dedicated, so shall the real presence of God fill the hearts of his people, and they "abide in" him as within temple-walls, forever holy and accepted. His kingdom shall be fully set up "within" his people, the hearts of these forming his throne. Surely, this is the glory to be "revealed in us."

It is difficult for those who are so prone to literalize even symbolic representations, and who have been so wont to think of the New Jerusalem as a picture of heaven itself, to look upon that exalted vision as an image of the church glorified, the "bride of Christ." Heaven is not his bride; the church is: and this is one with the New Jerusalem. All its glories form a rich and shining figure of the community of the saints in the great hereafter. The city is the simile of the church in its future holiness and security, its blessedness and worshipfulness; the "nations" walking in the light of this, the "kings" bringing their glory and honor into it, stand for the glorified saints in their social activities and all their endless life: the two—holy worship and heavenly occupations—blending forever through the never closed gates of the eternal city. The "nations" and "city" are interchangeable, and do not embrace two kinds of persons; for the gates of the city are forever open to all the residents of the new heavens and new earth. All the declarations of the Revelation point to only one class as having access to the city or composing this; while the church, radiant with heavenly splendor, shall be linked to all phases of that future and eternal life. "There shall in nowise enter into it anything that defileth, neither whatsoever worketh abomination, or maketh a lie: but they which are written in the Lamb's book of life."

III. We come now to the closing lines of the

Revelation from the ascended, living Jesus. One spirit has been awakened to a newer, and fuller, and stronger life in my own heart by my studies in this great portion of God's word; and that is, the spirit of *worship*. I trust this has been called forth, also, in yours. Reluctantly do I lay down the consideration of the subject. Not that! Nay, we will take this with us, in a broadened understanding and an enlarged heart, into all time to come, and be better prepared in mind for the coming realities of the future, and—I trust—for the "eternal weight of glory" in reserve for the redeemed. The spirit of worship was the chief thing excited in John as he looked upon the shining symbols and ministering angels. Whether his words, in the last chapter of the book, in relation to falling at the feet of the angel to worship, are a repetition of what he had once before stated; or, we are to understand that he had anew mistaken the angel, now personating Christ and conveying his message, for Christ himself, and had again prostrated himself in worship before such an one: certain is it that he was possessed, at the last of the visions, with a most fervent spirit of worship. Not permitted to worship an angel, even when speaking in the name of Christ; we do fall by faith at Jesus' feet and "Crown him Lord of all."

Words are now spoken which give us to know that beyond the finality of the things he has portrayed there is no other dispensation of grace to sinners. "He that is unjust, let him be unjust still: and he which is filthy, let him be filthy still: and he that is righteous, let him be righteous still: and he that is holy, let him be holy still." This is his closing argument: that, because of that unalterable condition of things which shall virtually come rapidly to each and all, and which in the whole sweep of · the ages—until Christ shall appear in unveiled reality—shall take place quickly, indeed, to the whole world, he would persuade us to be his disciples. He holds forth promise of reward, and warnings of justice; he declares his authority and endless power to bless and to punish, as the "Alpha and Omega, the beginning and the end, the first and the last." He urges the blessedness of those who "do his commandments"—or, as another rendering has it, "who wash their robes," "that they may have right to the tree of life, and may enter in through the gates into the city;" and he declares that "without are dogs, and sorcerers, and whoremongers, and murderers, and idolaters, and whosoever loveth and maketh a lie."

We remember Jesus in the days of his earthly life: in his pleadings—at times, his heart-broken pleadings with perverse men; when he wept over Jerusalem; when he lifted up his voice and cried: "If any man thirst let him come unto me." We think of his dying words of pity and love to sinners; and of his great commission of mercy: and, lo! once more his pleadings, once more his invitations, as "the root and offspring of David, and the bright and morning star"—the glory of the past and the hope of the future; the Messiah, the coming king; and he pleads with thee, at the last as at the first, with all who hear these words as with those who heard him when upon earth; and the riches of his love and anxiety to save your soul and give you a part in the glories of his church triumphant, the wealth of his atoning love and living grace, is crowded into one word—"Come!" Angel voices make tremulous the air with song of welcome; they sing to you, Come! and beckon you with white fingers to the land of purity and love: "Take heed how you hear." "The spirit in thy heart is whispering, Sinner, come!" with sweeter than syren voice is he wooing thee, not to destruction, but to endless life. The fair bride of Christ, on her way to the marriage feast, says to thee, Come! and offers thee from the bridegroom the wedding garment. The boatman stands on the shores of Time—washed forever with the waves of eternity—and calls after thee to bear thy hopes onward now, and thyself thither when the waters creep at thy feet chilling in death. See! as with rainbow tints God writes about the world of beauty, Come! Over the gates of the city of God is inscribed, "Whosoever will, let him come!" Above the door, and on either side, is placed in the blood of Christ—our Passover—the invitation, Come!

"The spirit and the bride say, Come! And let him that heareth say, Come! And let him that is athirst come. And whosoever will, let him take the water of life freely." You shall not say that you could not be saved. The great words of the infinite love of the infinite Jesus shall rise up to condemn you. Oh! if you are lost, if you at last are "cast into the lake of fire and brimstone," it shall be because "ye will not come" unto him that you may have life. Hear Jesus pleading with you as from heaven! See his outreached hands of love waiting to receive you! Fly as for thy life from the burning flood of hell to the arms of redeeming and glorifying mercy!

In his great love Jesus warns you against seeking or trusting any other way than that set forth in his word; of adding to, or taking from, the words of the book of this prophecy. The effort is being made to do so now. Attend, then, to the truth; that, in view of all these things, with your eternal life at issue, you are simply to "come to Christ," by humble, true, hearty, sin and world and self and satan-renouncing faith, to be saved by the righteousness and atoning merits of Jesus only.

Has Jesus said to us, "Come?" and have we come to Jesus? Then, when he says: "Surely, I come quickly. Amen;" we *will* respond, and *do* respond: "Even so, Come, Lord Jesus." That you may be aided to come, and prepared to bid him come; do I fervently exclaim, with the beloved John: "*The grace of our Lord Jesus Christ be with you all Amen.*"